THE PROSPE
OF CITIE

MW01296882

THE
CITYGATE

"Her husband is respected
at the city gate,
where he takes his seat
among the elders of the land."
(Proverbs 31:23)

JOHN KINGSLEY ALLEY

PEACE PUBLISHING

The City Gate,
Copyright © 2016 by John Kingsley Alley.

Published by:
Peace Publishing,
Rockhampton, Queensland, Australia.

Distributed in Australia by:
Peace Apostolic Ministries
PO Box 10187
Frenchville Qld 4701
Phone: 07 4926 9911
Email: mail@peace.org.au
Web: www.peace.org.au

Cover and interior design by Jonathan Maxwell, Peace Apostolic Ministries.

Unless otherwise indicated, all Scripture quotations are taken from the HOLY BIBLE,
NEW INTERNATIONAL VERSION. Copyright 1973, 1978, 1984 by International Bible
Society. Used by permission of Zondervan Publishing House. All rights reserved.

Scripture quotations marked KJV are taken from the King James Version of the Bible.

Scripture quotations marked YLT are taken from the Young's Literal Translation Version of
the Bible.

Scripture quotations marked NASB are taken from the NEW AMERICAN STANDARD
BIBLE®, Copyright © 1960,1962,1963,1968,1971,1972,1973,1975,1977,1995
by The Lockman Foundation. Used by permission.

Scripture quotations marked (ESV) are from The Holy Bible, English Standard Version®
(ESV®) Copyright © 2001 by Crossway, a publishing ministry of Good News Publishers.
All rights reserved. ESV Text Edition: 2011

Scripture quotations marked HCSB®, are taken from the Holman Christian Standard Bible®,
Copyright © 1999, 2000, 2002, 2003, 2009 by Holman Bible Publishers. Used by permission.
HCSB® is a federally registered trademark of Holman Bible Publishers.

That the Church may more fully be
the *'pure, chaste virgin'* for whom He died.

ACKNOWLEDGEMENTS

I wish to express my deep appreciation to the people of Peace Christian Church, Rockhampton, for the many years (28) of Christian love, fellowship, and service we have shared. Our people have supported me tirelessly, and many of us have shared thousands of prayer meetings together over the years (we typically have 15 prayer meetings a week). So many have gone out on ministry teams, too, and given so that others could go. The faithfulness and loyalty of the staff and people of Peace has been wonderful, and the love and support for the work always fresh and noble. They have continued to pray and believe year in and year out.

I have been greatly helped, too, and constantly encouraged and supported, by spiritual sons and other associates in many places, and I thank you sincerely. I have often said, if we have nothing else to offer the Body of Christ, we have this: that we love each other. And I have said to my staff, in one or two very difficult seasons, that if we lose everything, we will have still the best thing of all: we have each other.

I am helped more by my wife of 45 years, Hazel, than anyone. We often pray together, frequently without notice and at all hours, and she is most discerning. Her energy and work output, while always seeming to be fresh, is amazing to me. And she spends hours checking the manuscript of my books, not only for grammar and spelling errors, and readability, but also that we might doubly-ensure that the spirit and attitude conveyed is pure and above reproach. We do our best with that, it is very important to us.

Life for us at Peace is a team effort, lived in Christian love and community. We are, as the apostle said, *"members one of another"* (Romans 12:5 KJV).

CONTENTS

Introductions   Bob Bain

David Balestri

Doug Heck

George Johnson

Bob Bain

Pastor
Life Church COC,
Rockhampton, AUSTRALIA.

I first had contact with the church John Alley leads 25 years ago, when ministering at their Youth Conference. In 2007 I moved to Rockhampton to pastor Life Church. Since then John and I have had many prayers and coffees together and I have seen his ministry close-up. John and Hazel have a great family who love and serve God together with them, have built a great local church, and have 'sons' in ministry in many nations.

Like most Christian Leaders, John Alley has a life-goal desire to see our cities and nations won strongly for Christ. He and I along with other pastors here share a heart to see our city reached and God's people blessed. Recently, eight churches combined at Easter for Sunday morning worship.

I believe that what he shares in this book is a genuine understanding of how this can happen to a greater and more effective measure. Local church leaders must come to a place of standing together in love and spiritual authority in the cities God has called them to. For, where the *"brothers dwell in unity,"* there God commands *"the blessing"* (Psalm 133:1,3).

In the 1990s, I pastored a large church in a regional Queensland city for a 9-year period. During this time a great love and a heart for unity developed among the pastors in that city. A number of us grew closer, and this resulted in some regular combined public meetings that had great impact in the City. I believe it was this love and oneness that made all of us stronger, and even more effective in our individual churches.

As a direct result, one local denominational church that had experienced a split some 15 years previously, and which until then had been two small, struggling churches, was brought together. The restored church then quickly grew to become a large influential church in the city.

We found, too, a greater effectiveness in shepherding our flock, because of our open communications and flowing together.

Whatever our denominational affiliation may be, this understanding and its proposed out-workings truly deserves prayerful study and free and open discussion among those of us whose commitment to the Lord has brought us to the place of serving Him as leaders of local churches.

Bob Bain

David Balestri

Campus Pastor
Hope Unlimited Church,
Central Coast, Australia.

The thing that most impresses me about John Alley is that he is a practitioner of the word and the revelations he writes about, and not just a theorist. We have too many authors who have great ideals they espouse, and may genuinely aspire to, yet when you check their work on the ground amongst their family, congregations, and cities there seems to be a great disparity between proclamation and manifestation. This is not the reality with regards to John. Having had the honour to not only know John in conference settings but also having spent time in his family home and engaged with his leaders and church people, I am convinced that John is a man committed to "earthing" all that God has placed on his heart.

I have been saying to pastors and leaders in the Body of Christ all over the nation in the past couple of years that one of the greatest restorational truths that is upon us in this new season of apostolic reformation is the returning of the church to being primarily "apostolic in nature and prophetic in intent." This is of crucial importance if we are to see the Body of Christ rise to be the head and not the tail in the nations of the earth. The work can at times seem daunting and insurmountable and yet we thank God that in this hour, a fresh grace is being released upon the church.

What you will read in the following pages of this book is not simply a new program that we are to use as a patch to be sewn onto an old wineskin, but rather a key governmental principle and mega structure that the Body of Christ is meant to operate under across regions and territories. You will be provoked to think in contexts that may be larger than what you are used to or have been trained in, and yet, if you will prayerfully allow yourself to consider and embrace this dimension, I believe great ground will begin to be taken for the glory of God in your personal life, your ministry context, and also within your city.

David Balestri

Dr. Douglas Heck

Horizon Church
Seattle, WA,
U.S.A.

John,

I stand with you in prayer and the common goal toward city-eldership. We had such a sweet thing going for about 10 years here in Seattle, then it blew apart for various reasons. There were ten influential pastors meeting weekly for 2-3 hours, praying with one another, loving one another, and beginning to lead out. Then city-wide "old style" religious "events" encroached (big meetings) that were from the "outside," meaning special famous US speakers who tried to come to grab the city's attention. It was sad to see the distraction away from city-elder focus, and then to also watch all the resultant fleshly squabbles by those who wanted to jump in front of the parade and call it their own. In our ending months, a few pastors retired from ministry, some moved to other cities and ministries, one passed away, and three of us just stopped uniting and began doing our "own things." I am one who has tried to raise the banner once again, but finding resistance with similar reasons to those you mention. The end result broke my heart. Your vision gives me hope.

When I heard your sermon (via CD) on city eldership and the rains coming as you broke "claims" off cities, I took that as from God, and began to do that for Seattle and the Cascadia region. Things began to get better. Especially in the city regarding "distraction events." However, the plight for a city-eldership here is almost back to the beginnings again. I have looked to some of the younger emerging influential leaders, but found them generally lacking in necessary maturity to think regionally or Kingdom-wide.

Your book will be helpful. Please push through; we need what you carry inside of you.

I have your back,

Your friend,

Doug Heck

Dr. George D. Johnson

Harvest City Church
Vancouver, British Columbia,
Canada.

For over 50 years I worked to bring churches and fivefold ministries together within the context of the city. The ultimate goal has been to replicate the clear example of New Testament Christianity being set in a city as 'One Church.'

Without question, I have witnessed numerous breakthroughs resulting in tangible and visible outcomes. These were occasions where local churches and leaders, in some measure, had broken free from the frosty isolation of local denominational and sectarian spirit. Churches and leaders had come together with considerable effort and embraced in a small measure what it meant to be "One Church in the City."

I repeat, "small measure," because any and all efforts that I have witnessed have only been but a shadow of the power invested in the New Testament 'One City Church.' The Book of Acts beckons us to reach a new horizon. In the meantime we are thankful for all measures birthed by God, for these have the capacity to overcome the spirit of the world.

John Alley, in discussing City Eldership, has unlocked keys as to why so many efforts have been paralyzed and yielded only a "small measure."

In reading his book my spirit was stirred as I remembered a powerful encounter I had upon coming to Vancouver to pastor Harvest City Church some twenty-four years ago. One night, in a vivid and shocking dream, the Lord showed me the *chief demonic spirit* that resided over the City of Vancouver. In the dream I did my best to counter this Spirit, but to no avail. He did not defeat me, but I could not defeat him. It was a standoff.

This does not in any way diminish the fact that in the years that followed many wonderful churches were planted and numerous churches have grown, spiritually and numerically, to impact our city. As well, there have been numerous successful efforts of churches and leaders working together resulting in good fruit. I applaud all that God has done, is doing, and will do in the future of my city.

But what has remained a mystery to me over these many years is, Why the stand off in my encounter with the Dark Force? I now have come to see the significance of this book's teaching regarding the demonic empowerment that remains in its place whenever the church is fragmented rather than being spiritually one.

The author calls it "the corporate struggle with demonic power." To me this has been the missing link, so to speak. It isn't that we have not fought and contended with spiritual power in warfare whilst pursuing our Kingdom efforts. Rather it has been that we have not understood the seriousness of a fragmented Church within the city. Nor have we valued appropriately the potent power of a 'God-ordained City Eldership.'

I believe John Alley has not only given us this key, but other keys too, that will draw us closer to seeing our cities and nations being 'turned upside down' for God.

George D. Johnson

Author's Preface

My goal was to write a simple book, short enough for busy pastors to read easily, in the hope of raising the subject of a much needed conversation between us all. It was not intended that this book be an exhaustive reference or the final word, but rather something to shine light on some crucial subjects and to open the way for every believer's prayers, and for positive exploration by pastors and leaders. The result is larger than I had hoped, but in the end, the subject needed the full scope of all that is here.

The key subject that arises is eldership. You will find that wherever I use personal pronouns, I use 'he' exclusively for elders. There are several reasons. To begin with, the New Testament uses particularly exclusive language for the eldership role, and I have no warrant, no authority, to go beyond Scripture. I do allow for the fact that God does, in His dealings with us and history, make exceptions even to His own apparent way of normally doing things, but these exceptions are more rare than we might think, and usually done for particular, rather than general, reasons. However, I have covered well, I think, and given a positive and helpful view, on the more general question of women in ministry, in Chapter Six of my book, *The Apostolic Revelation*, and I need not go over that here. I also remember that General William Booth, founder of The Salvation Army, said, "My best men are women."

Aside from that, there are many in the Body of Christ, some denominations in particular, for whom referring to elders as both he and she inclusively is a false position as Bible doctrine, and I write for them as well. Women in churches everywhere are the most faithful, often the hardest working, and usually the most freely volunteering of all the saints. But with the wisdom of God, I have always taken the view in my own church that whilst everyone may participate in ministry, the wise application of that principle has been that women are *free* to participate, but the men must be *made* to participate. I knew that if I specifically required men to take leadership, the outcome would be that I would have strong men, and then have strong families with strong women and children, resulting in a strong church. But I knew that if we filled leadership vacancies on a volunteer basis, we would end up generally with weak men, and ultimately the church would deteriorate and become what it has become in many places in the West, a place for women and kids.

Eighty to ninety percent of all children who come to church end up like their dad. This has been proven statistically across the world in all cultures. It is because about 80% of our individual sense of identity, our sense of who we are and why we are here, comes from dad, right or wrong. Where dad is an unbeliever, but mum takes the children to church and faithfully seeks to raise them in the faith, most of them leave the church in their early teenage years and end up thinking and living like dad. But where dad is a believer and takes them to church, where he walks with God and sets an example, then even when his wife is an unbeliever, and even if she works against the faith, the great majority of the kids end up in the faith, same as dad. There is a case for greatly strengthening the men of the church, and this must include urging them into leadership responsibility. And there is a strong case that can be made for the eldership role to be exclusively reserved for those men who are the wisest and most mature of the spiritual fathers in ministry.

In the end, I am keeping the language of the book simple,

sticking with the gender language of the New Testament relative to eldership, and advising the reader who feels differently to not be offended by this but to apply the principles in accordance with your own conscience.

There will, no doubt, be some unanswered questions. For brevity, some aspects of the subject have not been explored. Rather, this book is meant to be an introduction to help everyone begin the faithful task of personally seeking the Lord, then that of praying with one another, and that of lengthy ongoing conversation and relationship development with one another, and of humility and submission to one another. That is how it should be, and needs to be, at this stage in the development of this subject in the Body of Christ across the world.

BUT THIS BOOK ALSO HIGHLIGHTS SOME BURNING ISSUES: There are areas of great ignorance, even among pastoral leaders, of very damaging spiritual conditions in the church, and fleshly attitudes and practices that empower demonic forces. There is bondage to be broken, and freedoms to be sought. Some of this is addressed, at least enough to awaken and make leaders everywhere alert to both the dangers and the vast opportunities before us in leading God's people into greater grace, and our cities into the blessings of the Kingdom of God.

I should mention that this subject was foreshadowed in Chapter Eight of my first book, *The Apostolic Revelation*, and a portion of the material in that chapter was revised for inclusion in Chapter Seven of this book.

I welcome any further inquiry from, or discussion with, other leaders in the Body of Christ.

With my love and sincere regards,

John Alley.

CHAPTER ONE

What Closed the Heavens?

*'Now Elijah... said to Ahab,
"As the Lord, the God of Israel, lives, before whom I stand,
there shall be neither dew nor rain these years,
except by my word." '*
(1 Kings 17:1)

*'After many days the word of the Lord came to Elijah,
"Go, show yourself to Ahab, and I will send rain upon the earth." '*
(1 Kings 18:1)

On Sunday, December 3, 2006, at home at Peace Christian Church in Rockhampton, I preached a message relative to the spiritual state of denominations and Christian institutions, not only in Australia but the world. I called it "The State of the War." It was good information, and one that people download from our website to this day. After a great morning of church fellowship, I went home at peace in the Lord, had a good lunch, and took a nap.

But I had a growing feeling that the Lord was asking me to go out that night, drive around Rockhampton, and pray for each of the churches. I was to pray in accordance with the need I had expressed in the morning. And what I prayed for others, I was to pray for our own church.

I took with me my eldest son, David, one of our key leaders, who was at the time the pastor of our Mt. Morgan church. We drove to each church, one after another, where we paused for just a minute or so to take authority over something that was established in the spirit realm and hindering them. Each prayer needed no more than 30 seconds. The outing took about two hours, and I went home.

But within an hour the unexpected happened. In the midst of severe drought across several states, and contrary to the forecast, the weather changed! But only over our city.

———————

Before I tell you of the events about to unfold, please consider the following:

Rain, and in its absence, drought, is often used in the Scriptures as the symbol of an open or a closed heaven, respectively. This biblical concept of the heavens being open or closed is meant to communicate a spiritual reality, such as: God is or isn't pleased with His people; His people have turned away from the Lord to serve other gods; His people are not listening; there may be a build-up of established reproaches of sin against the Church in the nation; or, they have hardened their hearts and their worship is only outward observance with their hearts focused on other loves, they cling to traditions taught by men not God, and they've long since stopped seeking after righteousness. In cases like these, there may in fact be much religion in the land, 'Christian' religion, but very little listening and walking with God in humility.

We have an example of the use of these symbols with the story of Elijah and Ahab in 1 Kings 16-18. Through Elijah the Lord closed the heavens, but when the great breakthrough came on Mount Carmel with the victory of Elijah over the prophets of Baal, the weather afterward changed as a direct outcome. Within no time there was a huge cloudburst. Normal weather patterns resumed, and the blessing they brought on the economy returned.

More clearly, in the Lord's famous declaration to Solomon, He revealed precisely these great realities; *"When I shut up the heavens so that there is no rain... if my people, who are called by my name, will humble themselves and pray and seek my face and turn from their wicked ways, then I will hear from heaven, and I will forgive their sin and will heal their land"* (2 Chronicles 7:13-14).

Rain, and the abundance and prosperity it produces, as against drought, and the hardship, struggle, and economic decline that comes with it, are not necessarily signs of the spiritual state of the nation, but of the church!

And these are not just symbols! In the Bible it is not just the *terminology* of rain and drought that is used as an illustration of spiritual truth. Rather, *actual* drought and rain are present, as curse or blessing, being physical and economic indicators of spiritual reality. When there were serious spiritual problems in the land, there really was drought, and when there was faithfulness, there really was rain.

These then are powerful symptoms, as much now as they were then, of spiritual realities in the day-to-day affairs of God's dealings with His people. As such, they are not simply interesting word pictures, they are in fact clear object lessons, present as prophetic signs, and showing up as realities in the daily construct of life and the economy.

These are not the only indicators, either; but it is a good place to start.

The Drought We Had

Now back to my story. Up until that time we had known almost nothing but drought for many years, and by now this extended all down Eastern Australia. Things were particularly severe, with all of New South Wales, most of Queensland, and much of Victoria 'drought declared.' I remember driving though N.S.W. on my way to South Australia, and hour after hour you would not see a cow or a sheep in those bare paddocks – and at home, the grass of my lawn was dead, and so dry that when you walked on it, it would crunch under your feet.

Locally in Central Queensland, it seemed as if we'd had 15 years of continuous drought, although in reality it was one period of drought after another. This was late 2006, but I can remember how often in the 1990s we prayed on many Sundays for rain – and almost always got refreshing showers, but without breaking the drought.

But in the 2000s, on our home property, the dam dried up and the ground was parched and brown, for there had been no rain in a long time. At our country house we were totally dependent on tank water, which had to come from either rain or the dam. God was good to us, for through the worst of the drought, when month in, month out, there was not enough rain to turn a single blade of grass green, He put a shower on our roof every two weeks or so, so that our tank never ran dry. A 5,000 gallon tank of water lasted only 3 weeks at our house – but in the 18 months of that bad drought, our tank never ran dry, and we never had to buy water.

But on Sunday night 3rd December, 2006, within one hour of going home after David and I had prayed for each church, the weather changed over the city. Unforecast, unexpected, seemingly out-of-nowhere, a storm arose – a wonderful storm. It was not destructive, yet it poured over our city, and on my home and property north of the city. And following on from that, we then had rain events about four times a week, for months, but only over our city. Much of the state of Queensland remained in drought, but Rockhampton became an island of green in an ocean of drought.

In the following year or two I shared the story of this prayer and its dramatic outcome with pastors here and there, some of whom prayed the same kind of prayer over their localities. And guess what? It rained there too. Ballarat, in Victoria, was one of those places, and Lake Wendouree, a huge feature in the city that had completely dried out from drought, filled again. I have since stood on the shore of that beautiful lake, dressed in my tuxedo, and participated in the lovely wedding of a young couple, who were both of families from Zimbabwe.

A year or two later, conducting a live-in ministry training school for pastors and leaders at Emu Park, Qld, I shared about the prayer over the Rockhampton churches and the weather outcome. In attendance was a denominational pastor from Southern N.S.W. who related a similar occurrence. At the height of the drought, he felt led by the Lord to walk around his town and pray a certain kind of prayer concerning each of the churches. He reported that the drought then immediately broke over his community, whilst the rest of New South Wales remained in drought. His town, too, had become an island of green in that sea of drought.

What was his prayer? **What did the Lord tell him to say? And,** *what was my prayer?* What kind of prayer, so brief as to take a mere 30 seconds, repeated over all the denominations and independent churches as well, could bring this kind of dramatic outcome – and in the one thing that is the biblical sign of an open or closed heaven?

The answer to these questions is what this book is about. And as we go forward, you will discover not only what the point of these prayers was, but why they are so needed.

However, a further adventure and discovery in prayer was about to unfold, the implications of which we will come to later in the book. The sequence of events began just over two years later, in 2009, when I asked one of the ladies in the church, Dr. Lynda Lorraway, if she would devote herself to seeking the Lord with a question. She was a person who had on other occasions presented key insights in prayer, so I thought I should give her the specific task of prayerfully obtaining an objective, independent viewpoint. The question I proposed was, *"What*

do we need to do to get the final breakthrough for the city?"
And I told the church I had given her this assignment.

It took time in prayer, but some months later Lynda came to me with what the Lord gave her, and on the basis of her insight (which I deal with later) I began to pray over Rockhampton. Her word from the Lord was: **"The old eldership is resisting the new eldership."** Not what I was expecting. How relevant could that be? I thought at first I knew what it meant, thinking it only referred to the history of our own church. But as I prayed into it, I saw it was, spiritually, a huge matter.

Two weeks later I was to take a long road trip of 5,000 kilometres with Hazel and our three youngest children from Rockhampton to Ballarat, then on to Melbourne and back. We would pass through many cities, towns, and villages.

I said to Hazel, "If this prayer is so important for Rockhampton, then it's important everywhere. Let's pray this way for every town we pass through." During three days of driving through Queensland, New South Wales, and Victoria, we stopped the car at every town, got out, planted our feet on the ground, and prayed for the church of that community in accordance with the prayer we had previously offered for the churches of Rockhampton, combined with the new insight I had from Lynda as well. The two were clearly parts of a greater whole.

What happened? We prayed our way south through Mt. Morgan, Banana, Theodore, Miles, and numerous other places to Goondiwindi, then on to Moree and Narrabri the first day. On the second, we went on through Coonabarabran and Gilgandra to Dubbo, and then through many inland N.S.W. towns until by mid-afternoon we were in Young, famous for cherries. There, praying under the great tree outside the downtown Information Centre, formerly the Railway Station, Hazel heard the Lord speak, shared it with me, and wrote it in her journal. The Lord said, *"As a result of these prayers, water will flow down the*

Murray/Darling rivers again.” This was in early December, 2009.

Not far into 2010 great rain events did begin, two in particular, that put huge flows down the enormous and iconic river system that had become Australia's greatest ecological disaster, the Murray/Darling Rivers.

But meanwhile, back in Young, we finished our prayers and continued on our way, praying over many more communities. After ministry in Victoria we came home for a busy new year and promptly forgot all about the word the Lord had given us concerning the rivers. We had not realised the significance of what we had been told.

Almost a year later, in November 2010, while we were at home praying one Saturday evening, outside heavy rain was pelting down, making wonderful music on our metal roof. In the middle of my prayer I started to thank the Lord for the rain, when suddenly it occurred to me that I ought to give thanks to the Lord for the huge flows of water that had flowed during the year down the Murray/Darling. Lake Eyre was full, the Menindee Lakes had recovered – it was wonderful! These were great and rare occurrences. As Hazel heard me pray about this, she remembered that somewhere we had a word from the Lord about that, and while I prayed on, she opened the sideboard and got out her notes, looking for what was just a vague memory. And there it was, from 11 months before in Young: *“As a result of these prayers, water will flow down the Murray/Darling rivers again.”*

We were scheduled to go again to Ballarat and Melbourne just two weeks later. I said to Hazel, “These prayers are obviously much more significant than we realise. When we do the trip in two weeks, let's pray this all over again – this time with more faith and purpose.” (This time with feeling!)

For this second prayer trip, in December 2010, I decided we

needed to pray not only for the towns we drove through, but also for every town we saw named on a signpost, no matter how distant. Neither did we stop and stand as before. We had far more extensive prayers for each place to get through, and we prayed continuously the whole time we were driving. I would pray, then Hazel, then back to me – the big advantage of having only two people in a prayer meeting is everyone knows whose turn it is to pray next! Altogether we prayed for three days to Ballarat, a further two half-days into Melbourne and on to Phillip Island and back, and then three days home. For the return we took a different route, up through Yass, Canberra, Goulburn, and Sydney, on to Newcastle, and then along the whole of the North Coast of N.S.W. with its many towns, into the Gold Coast and Brisbane, the Sunshine Coast, and then north along the east coast of Queensland. We continued in prayer over the many cities and towns, such as Gympie, Maryborough, Hervey Bay, Childers, Bundaberg, Gladstone, and all the numerous villages and towns named on signs, until finally home. This was six full days and two half-days of continuous prayer over much of Eastern Australia. The Holy Spirit must have helped us.

The result? As we were leaving Rockhampton and commenced to pray, it began to rain behind us. It followed us down the highway, pursuing us it seemed, until finally it overtook us. It rained throughout Queensland and down through N.S.W. Then huge rains came over Victoria, and we only just got out ahead of the floods. As we drove up the East coast, the rains kept coming and the weather closed in.

We got home ahead of most of it, about mid-December, and what followed was extensive flooding all along Eastern Australia. The outcome was incredible: the year just ended, 2010, of which the Lord had said during our prayers of December 2009 that "Water will flow...," became the third wettest year in Australian records. But the year that followed our second prayer journey, 2011, became the second wettest year in Australian records.

In Rockhampton, we were cut off from all outside transport, road, rail, and air, for two weeks. The airport was closed for three weeks, covered with water for two, and we had to fly our own aircraft (Peace Aviation) out ahead of the floodwaters and park them on country strips. And we were cut off from our church property for three weeks. It was high and dry, but there was no road access because of floodwater.

Why was there so much water given at that time, more, you would think, than needed. Because we had two ecological problems, not just the one of the river system I have already described. The other was that under the continent of Australia is a huge artesian basin, i.e. underground water. But it had been hugely depleted. It needs huge rain and floods to renew the aquifer. What was the Lord doing? He was healing the land.

What kind of prayer so addresses the spiritual issues over the nation that this kind of thing can be the sudden outcome? What is it that has so bound the church that serious consequences damage the nation and keep it in bondage? And what is this spiritual disorder that, when addressed with authority, we then see great shifts take place in the heavenly realms over the nation, with immediate affects on the weather in the first instance?

Later in the book, I will tell you more specifically what was prayed. In every case, it had to do with entrenched religion and tradition in Christianity. But I cannot do this without first setting out the teaching of Chapters Two to Seven, in which I give the necessary biblical and spiritual context needed to understand the relevance of the prayers.

After these prayers the changes we saw were dramatic, but not everlasting – because the problem had not been permanently removed, simply pushed back temporarily.

This book seeks to offer the more permanent solution.

Official Weather Records

The following quotations are taken from the website of the Australian Government Bureau of Meteorology, and may be found at this link: http://www.bom.gov.au/climate/enso/history/ln-2010-12/rainfall-flooding.shtml

"In 2010, Australia experienced its third-wettest year since national rainfall records began in 1900, with second place taken by 2011. Averaged across Australia, both years experienced rainfall well above the long-term average of 465 mm – 703 mm in 2010 and 708 mm in 2011."

"2010 was also the wettest year on record for the Murray– Darling Basin"

"While the 2010–11 La Niña event was costly in an economic and social sense, it relieved one of the longest and most severe droughts across the Murray– Darling Basin in recorded history. Heavy rain provided a significant boost to water storages in Queensland, New South Wales and South Australia."

"Combined, the two events yielded Australia's wettest 24-month period on record (April 2010 to March 2012), and wettest two-calendar year period (2010–2012)."

Widespread flooding

"The record-breaking rainfall during the 2010–11 La Niña led to widespread flooding in many regions between September 2010 and March 2011. As well as the severe flooding in southeast Queensland, large areas of northern and western Victoria, New South Wales, northwestern Western Australia and eastern Tasmania were subject to significant flooding. There were also some highly unseasonable rain events in the tropics during what is typically its dry season.

"Flooding was also widespread during the 2011–12 La Niña. Much of inland southern and far northern Queensland, most of New South Wales, northern Victoria, and central Australia experienced flooding at least once between late November 2011 and March 2012."

CHAPTER TWO

Our In-House Eldership Journey

*"And when they had appointed elders for them in every church,
with prayer and fasting they committed them to the Lord
in whom they had believed."*
(Acts 14:23 ESV)

It was as a Salvation Army Officer that I came to Rockhampton, Central Queensland, in 1986. But late the following year, the church that became my home, known at that time as Peace Memorial Baptist Church, asked me to become their pastor and lead them into renewal. I sought the Lord earnestly, for I was also being offered a major promotion where I was, and after weeks of prayer saw clearly what I was to do. I became their minister in January, 1988.

Rockhampton is a city in the tropics on the East coast of Australia, which back then had a population of less than sixty thousand people, and about forty churches. Most of these were traditional denominational churches. Spiritually the city was quite dark, we were to discover, and a city Australians generally didn't visit. If they where travelling from Brisbane on their way North, they would drive as far as Rockhampton, stop the night, then go on their way. Few ever stayed and holidayed. It seemed a grey, drab, rundown kind of place, and seemed to have a feeling of heaviness. It was arguably one of Australia's harder places to minister, especially if one was looking to make greater progress.

Peace Baptist, though, was a happy place, and spiritually hungry, but did not know a lot about renewal; so I began teaching on faith and prayer. It became the norm to see many wonderful and miraculous healings. After a year I taught about the baptism of the Holy Spirit and the proper place of speaking in tongues, and the whole church stepped into a fuller experience of life in the Holy Spirit. We had a delightful journey into greater heights of worship and prayer, and the church was full of joy and faith. We must have been given much grace, because in the days of the charismatic movement that kind of thing had often divided churches.

A Call to Prayer

We began to pray much for the city. Really, a call to prayer was our sense of what we were meant to be about. The truth is, we didn't know all that much about how to do anything greater as a church, but we knew we were to pray, so that's what we did. As we prayed for the city we began to see it change, and the City Council did a great deal at that time, and since, to beautify the city. Rockhampton began to be renewed, and wealth began to grow.

However the city had been under extensive curses. A visiting English novelist, Anthony Trollope, passed through the region in 1871, and is credited with being the originator of the declaration that Rockhampton was "the city of sin, sweat, and sorrow."[1] That he personally authored it is debatable, even though he has the renown for it, but the local newspaper, the *Rockhampton Bulletin*, had used similar terminology earlier, and then published the declaration about the city without reference to Trollope, on 6th November, 1875. Either way, spiritually it was a real and dreadful curse. It is said, too, that one of Australia's renowned poets, Banjo Paterson, further declared the statement over the city in verse, which I can't confirm, but certainly a

---

1 https://www.nla.gov.au/behind-the-scenes/2012/10/29/the-city-of-sin-sweat-sorrow-trollope-and-rockhampton

history of the region published by the local university is called *Sin, Sweat and Sorrow: the Making of Capricornia Queensland 1840s-1940s*. Thus all that time Rockhampton was known by this epithet, "the city of sin, sweat, and sorrow."

We were to discover, however, with time and progress in prayer, that this curse was not the only one. Other greater curses were also at work. But this was where we began. It's been a step-by-step process, and at times a tremendous battle, through many years of both struggle and progress.

In the process we were to learn a lot about walking with each other as well as with God. The Lord gave us breakthroughs and brought us into wonderful graces with respect to walking in relationship with each other. As a result our people became a people who loved each other, out of which came the writing of my earlier books.

The 'Old' Eldership

When I first came to Peace, it was a Baptist church with congregational government that held a quarterly members' meeting and a monthly deacons' meeting. Prior to my commencement the church had no minister for over 12 months, but the Deacons would meet monthly, and the meetings would go very late, often until midnight, trying to sort out church needs and business. I opted for a different approach.

I established a weekly meeting with firm guidelines. We would meet at 6p.m. Tuesdays, and everyone would fast for the meeting. Secondly, at this regular meeting we would pray for a minimum of one hour. We could pray longer, but until we had done so, no business would be discussed. Thirdly, no meeting would be allowed to go late – all meetings would finish within two hours or so. And fourthly, since everyone present had accepted nomination to be a deacon, that meant that each had accepted the responsibility of being a leader. For spiritual leadership, two things were so basic they were universally required – a spiritual leader prays, and a spiritual leader is a financial giver. I always made it clear that it was the duty of each one to personally get the victory in those two specific matters. Otherwise they could not in any real sense see themselves as a spiritual leader.

The Tuesday meetings quickly became quite profound as prayer meetings. I was aided by the fact that a few of those older Baptist men were strong in prayer and faith, and the rest soon learned. It was wonderful each year to see newly-elected leaders begin timid in faith but within a few weeks or months powerfully interceding with passion, along with the rest.

The other great result was that after we had prayed for an hour or more, and sometimes a good deal longer, once we turned to business nothing ever seemed too difficult, and decisions were made quickly and easily. Grace sees to this. It was common to finish the meeting at 7.30p.m. And our Sundays were powerfully blessed as well.

But previously the church had some history of division. Consequently there was a culture of wariness, and in practice, elected leadership was not afforded any great amount of trust. The deacons had no authority to actually make decisions, rather they made recommendations to the members' meeting, where everything was voted on. If a tyre on the church bus was unroadworthy, it couldn't be replaced without a vote from the members' meeting.

It was necessary to improve on that, and fortunately I was given the love and trust of the congregation. Before long, we decided to revise the constitution, and to establish four levels of church administration where decisions could be made based on relative authority. One of the steps I proposed to the church as being biblically important – essential in my mind at that time – was to establish an eldership.

I assumed, in keeping with the practice common in many

churches, that elders were to be found amongst the men who were the spiritually mature, respected, and trustworthy senior believers in the congregation, and that these should stand with the minister to be the accountable spiritual leaders, in a team, over the congregation. This belief is what we acted on.

The four levels of decision-making this gave us were these: the Senior Minister, the Eldership, the Church Council, and the Members' Meeting, each with their own clearly defined roles and decision-making authority. This gave us very good outcomes for quite a long time.

However, about ten years earlier the church had split over this very question of eldership. Fifty families had gone one way and thirty families another. But when I presented the case for a better way of governing the church, a more biblical one, I thought, it was unanimously supported. This breakthrough changed the culture of the church, and in the following eleven years of members' meetings, until and including the time we adopted an entirely new Constitution that removed congregational government, we had unanimous members' decisions for almost every decision that was taken. A great deal of grace was given to us in those days in seeking to pursue the will of God. But the unity since established by our breakthroughs has been much greater.

As a result of the changes the Church Council expanded in number, and was now comprised of the elders and deacons, the other pastors on staff that we had added because of growth, and myself.

I had personally identified the initial elders, and proposed them to the church, which then voted for them. And things went very well for a good while. We had good relationships, there was a high level of respect and trust, and many of us became close friends. We met weekly for strong prayer, but also held regular Church Council Prayer retreats, when we would go away after work on Friday and spend most of the weekend seeking the Lord and praying for the church.

It wasn't long before it became obvious that, as a church, we were greatly enjoying what was an extended protection and spiritual covering over the people as a whole. It was clear that the grace the Lord had given me to lead the church was now being extended through the love, unity, and prayer of this team of people. Church life was quite wonderful, with a lot of joy in the house, healings, and progress in all kinds of things including finance and property.

There were challenges as well as opportunities, but these were very happy years. The church grew, and we extended the building. We began sending teams on international ministry. Our youth numbers expanded rapidly, and our youth meetings saw as much grace with worship, healings, and converts, as our Sunday services. We sold the church property and developed a new multi-million dollar property on 25 acres. And we commenced a Christian school and a Bible College.

Division in the Eldership

However, seven years later and established in our new property, there arose a division in the eldership. This broke the covering that had been so effective, and we found ourselves under spiritual opposition. Up until that time we had enjoyed a high level of protection over our people – but when the covering broke, we had a flood of destroying spirits enter the church. (My understanding is that 'covering' is not just accountability and belonging, but more – it has a spiritual power dimension, i.e. it is a grace, an anointing that is effectively a spiritual force-field.[2])

The result was that we became very busy, run off our feet with pastoral care. Up until then we had not had struggles within the marriages in the church, but we began to find some couples coming under pressure. And we had strange manifestations of sicknesses that needed prayer. I remember once being called in the middle of the night by parents requesting prayer, because

2 For a biblical discussion of this, see Chapter 7 of my book, *The Apostolic Revelation*.

they had found their child with a lot of blood all over the pillow, and no reason could be found for it.

How did such eldership division arise? It was in fact initiated by the wives of three of the elders acting outside all authority, and it came out of something that shouldn't have become an issue. The background was that we had received a visiting speaker one Sunday morning, a lady who upheld traditional family values, and in the process was very honouring of larger families and home schooling – things that are dear to many, and which in no sense are evil. But for some reason one woman in particular was apparently determined to correct what she saw as a terrible and unbalanced emphasis.

Thus it was that these three ladies wrote a long letter to the church, taking up these issues, criticizing the speaker, and in a confrontational way insisting that their spiritual opinions were the correct ones for the church. The letter did not mention me, or anyone in the church, or anything I had said or taught, yet it was nevertheless a direct undermining of all leadership and authority in the house. The letter was handed out personally to every woman in the church on a Sunday morning when I was away preaching in a nearby town for the morning. And their husbands, three of the elders, knew all about it, but did not advise the rest of the eldership what was being done.

At no time had any of these women raised any aspect of the matter for discussion, not with me, nor another pastor, nor the elders or the Church Council. No concern was ever expressed to the leadership, which meant the eldership had no idea there was a variance of opinion to be considered. Instead, unilateral action was taken to assert control over the church. It was an extremely foolish act on their part, but as in the Garden of Eden, the great fault was with their husbands, who were elders but did not keep faith with their brothers, and so broke the covering. These three elders knew their wives were acting behind the backs of the pastors and the eldership, and were compliant, and therefore complicit, in it.

I returned that evening to discover the situation, but did not realise the implications. I knew it was out of order, but thought we could quietly work it through and resolve the issues. But instead, over time things became more and more difficult with those couples, and then with some others in the church, for they had opened the door to forces of division they didn't understand.

It is not necessary to our subject to labour the story here. What followed was a very difficult two-year period in which all our hearts were tested – yet it seemed the Lord had intended it, to refine the church as a whole, for a greater purpose. But as I look back and think about what was behind that and some of the other things that happened, I realise that very often people act without knowing the motive of their own hearts. In this case, it was not really about promoting balance on the named issues raised in the letter at all, and the action was not for the benefit of other believers.

The result, however, was that the church was let down badly by a few, and it resulted in a serious testing time for everyone, because once the spiritual oversight of a church allows division *in themselves*, it opens the door to a restless evil, and the spirit of that enters into the greater church. This is why we found we had increasing division from other directions within. This very painful process took over two years to work through, and in the end these former leaders and some other members left the church.

At the time what I didn't understand was that much of the root cause of our problems actually lay in the *system* – ie, with the *kind* of eldership we had established. And of course, I was keen to rebuild the good we had before. Since we were left with a smaller group of elders, for me it meant we had to re-form and strengthen that eldership so as to re-establish the strength of the covering.

We did raise new people to the eldership, and continued to meet and pray as always. But whilst the fellowship of the group was good, and we were greatly at peace with one another, the eldership seemed to lack power. It never seemed to have quite the grace that it had before. I was constantly holding up before the Lord an enquiry about what to do. Two things were to come out of that enquiry.

The first was that we needed to recognize and establish an apostolic covering over the church. That is, I and my team and our people were to relate personally and spiritually to a mature minister of Christ who had longevity, maturity, and apostolic grace as a spiritual father – first of all to me, but also to the church as a whole. This had nothing to do with whether we were in a denomination or not – in fact we were still very active and committed in the denomination at that time – it had to do with putting relational, spiritual oversight in place. The kind that had fathering grace and apostolic authority.[3]

A Different Kind of Eldership?

The second thing that came out of my enquiry of the Lord regarding the powerlessness of the old eldership was that I began to have a strong inner sense that the eldership we had was not the kind of eldership the Bible speaks of. I began to sense that there was something very wrong with it, that somehow it was not biblical, not in keeping with New Testament Christianity. But I could not see why.

Despite this lack of understanding, I continued to be assured by inner witness of the Holy Spirit that Christ was going to be bringing in a *new kind* of eldership. I didn't have a clue what it was, didn't know what it could look like, in fact I couldn't imagine *any* different kind of eldership other than what we had. Nevertheless, the conviction continued that Christ was about to do this – and that we needed to set aside our old eldership to make way for the new. It seemed clear that if we clung to the old it would be a roadblock to what the Lord had for us. We

---

3 I cover this subject in other books, namely *The Apostolic Revelation* and *The Spirit of Sonship.*

needed to get it out of the road to help prepare for what the Lord wanted to do.

We had eight elders, four who were full-time staff and four others. So, in the year 2000, these eight elders and their wives met in my house and discussed all this together. I proposed that this old style of managing the church was like a bottle with a skinny neck, and that the eldership style we had slowed down the good things that were meant to be poured out of us. I suggested that instead, we needed to open it up, and develop a new broad-based kind of leadership for our church (for dedicated local leadership standing with pastors is hugely important). I also suggested that, since we believed that the Lord had a different kind of eldership in mind, we needed to respond to the leading of the Spirit and close the old one down.

Sixteen people in that room were agreed; this was what they also believed the Lord was saying to us. We took a vote, a unanimous one, to close the eldership. We agreed we would raise new and more leaders, develop a broad-based consensus style of leadership within the congregation, and look to the Lord to lead us in the understanding of a different kind of eldership, one that was not just for us but for the whole Body of Christ.

CHAPTER THREE

Discovering the 'New' Eldership

"The reason I left you in Crete
was that you might put in order what was left unfinished
and appoint elders in every town,
as I directed you."
(Titus 1:5 NIV)

Within a year I had three formative experiences I was not looking for. They eventuated in the way that God has of educating you and getting you to see and understand new things.

Formative Experience #1 – A Prophetic Word and some Nasty Opposition

I was invited to Brisbane to speak to a gathering of Uniting Church pastors interested in renewal. We met in a classroom, and there were a number of other people present as well. At the end of the day the spontaneous occurred. We closed the meeting, but a young lady in her 20s who had left to go home returned five minutes later to speak with me personally. She was a member of a Uniting Church, and someone unusually gifted with prophetic discernment. She said she had a word for me, and felt compelled to return to share it.

"The Lord says He wants you to pray to understand *the fabric of the fivefold*, then you will understand what is coming against you through your school," she said.

Of course she didn't know we had a school. And she didn't know that our church and I were being opposed by something invisible but very strong and entrenched in our city. And I didn't realise, until then, that it was coming primarily through the school.

But we do have a school, which I founded in 1993, and I am glad to report that after the struggles I will report here, it has gone on to do very well. But as I look back, I realise in hindsight that indeed the troubles aimed at us by principalities and powers got most of their access via the school. But how could that be? The school was under the same covering as the church, and many of the school staff were our own people, including the Principal and all the School Board. What was the vulnerability?

The school had started exceptionally well, but then, following on from the entrance of division into the eldership, big problems arose. That spirit of division affected school staff more than anyone else associated with the church, with a bitterness that was targeted against the church. Some staff in particular were full of sullen and unreasoning accusations against the church and its leaders, whilst arguing the school's exclusive merits. I explained to them, in a staff meeting, "Your vilification will not destroy the church – it will only work to destroy the school." They could not be reasoned with (admittedly there was a most powerful principality of deception at work), and what I predicted turned out to be the case. Within a year or so, the school (which was under an independent board and chair) collapsed to very few students and staff, and I stepped in to rebuild it. It would have been easier to close it, but Christ wanted that school.

Yet the next few years were difficult. Like the church, there was now peace amongst the school community, but we were to go through several years where we couldn't seem to get ahead no matter how hard we tried, both in the school and the church. We would take a step forward, but always seemed to get knocked back. We survived, and we enjoyed each other and the Lord, but we couldn't seem to grow. And there was always the burden of being opposed. What was it that we were struggling with? What hated us so much that we were sorely opposed? It was at this point that the young lady with the prophecy spoke of the need to seek understanding of the "fabric of the fivefold."

One day, one of the mothers in the church came to see me. This sister had a Christian Outreach Centre background and was used to the idea of personal intercession and getting words of knowledge and prophecy. She had a story to tell me. She had been deep in prayer, offering strong intercession for the school, when she had a very frightening experience. She said that suddenly, as if rising out of the sewer from under the school, there came at her a ferocious, angry, destroying spirit full of vitriolic hatred and murderous lust. She said she recoiled in horror, that the matter was too big for her, and she wasn't going back there in prayer again.

It was obviously worse than I had thought. But this did confirm that powerful destructive forces were lined up against us, and that somehow the school was a major focal point of the attack.

I cannot divulge too much of what we went on to discover, but when I got to the bottom of it, after almost a decade of pain, it turned out that it was the hatred of another of the ministers in the city, toward our school in particular, that was giving unfettered authority and power to a spiritual principality.

I came to realise that it was from the time I had started the school, about five years after I had commenced leadership at Peace, that I began to feel less joy and more weariness in the work. Up until then it had been a delight. It turned out that this was where the real opposition in the spirit realm was focused, activated by the condemnation and strong, fleshly judgements of another pastor.

Words are deadly. So are fleshly thoughts and attitudes that we project against one another. Paul commanded us to *"bless and do not curse"* (Romans 12:14), and further informed, *"If you keep on biting and devouring each other, watch out or you will be destroyed by each other"* (Galatians 5:15). All this is even more critical, devastatingly evil, when at work amongst the ministers of Christ.

Not everyone is familiar with, or likes to use the term, "the fivefold ministry." But it is a term commonly used across much of the Body of Christ to designate the ordained leadership of the church in terms of Ephesians 4:11, where it says, *"Christ gave some to be apostles, some to be prophets, some to be evangelists, and some to be pastors and teachers."* In using this term, we are referring to the ministers that Christ has appointed to be the leaders of His Body. It is a useful term for this purpose, which is why it is so commonly used.

My understanding is this. When Christ appoints someone to the fivefold ministry, whether apostle, prophet, evangelist, pastor, or teacher, He has appointed them to represent Himself in leadership to the Body. Because the very purpose for which He anoints them is to represent Christ in leadership to the church, they have what we might call the Christ anointing – an anointing unique to those so appointed.

We should note that such appointments, if from Christ, are to the Body of Christ, not to a denomination or a specific sectarian interest. This is significant. A Lutheran pastor is not appointed by Christ to be the pastor of a Lutheran congregation, but to be one of the pastors to the city. A Baptist pastor does not carry an anointing just for the small segment of the Body of Christ in the city known as a congregation, but rather is anointed to represent Christ to the whole city and to the whole Body. And in this role, as a Christ appointment, each is part of a greater whole.

There is but one Body of Christ. Even though we meet in many locations under various leaders, properly understood we are one. We are spiritually joined, and this joining is real. We are *"members together of one body"* (Ephesians 3:6). There is but one *"golden lampstand"*[1] for the city.

The phrase supplied to me in the young lady's prophecy, 'the fabric of the fivefold,' I had not heard before. But it is quite graphic, and becomes self-explanatory. All of those appointed to the fivefold ministry of any given location are knitted together, whether they know it or not. The term 'fabric' speaks of a garment, and this garment is none other than the spiritual covering placed over the Body of Christ by the ministry of the anointed fivefold ministers the Lord appoints. And this covering affects the Body powerfully.

The 'fabric of the fivefold' implies that we are joined as one garment, and indeed we are. And what one pastor does – or says – affects all the others. And this works both negatively and positively, that is, for both blessing and cursing.

When the pastor of one denomination thinks little of another, speaks disparagingly of them, or just has no regard or respect for them, this is a case of someone with a Christ anointing cursing another person with the Christ anointing. This is the equivalent of Christ cursing Christ. And this is why the Body of Christ is so weak and ineffective, and so bound by religious and traditional spirits.

But when we all know one another, honour each other, love one another deeply from the heart, willingly serve and lay down our lives for each other, and guard each other's honour, then does the freedom and joy of the church increase. And doing these things for each other is commanded in Holy Scripture.[2] How much more than our church members should the ministers of Christ be doing these things toward *each other*.

On numbers of occasions over the years I have had to defend myself, my family, or the people of God, by taking a stand in prayer to cut off the spirit of witchcraft coming against us

---

1 Revelation 1:12,20, 2:1.
2 Romans 12:10-11, Galatians 5:13, Ephesians 5:21, 1 Thessalonians 5:11, Hebrews 10:25

because of some brother or sister's jealousies, fears, insecurity, criticisms, denunciations, or gossip, often expressed in various ways within their own circles or their own homes. When other ministers or church leaders do this, they are cursing the Body, and it is necessary to annul the cursing. This does not mean cursing them; no, we forgive and love them, but it does mean cutting off the power of their 'curses,' and resolutely dealing with the demonic spirits of witchcraft which their words and attitudes have, unknown to them, given authority and power to.

But we have this kind of problem all over the Body of Christ, because very few understand the fabric of the fivefold. Most do not realise just how joined they are, nor act out of much conviction that the Body is one.

Formative Experience #2 – No Titles, Happy Leaders

I went as the guest speaker for a weekend to a church in the Northern suburbs of Brisbane. It was a Pentecostal church of about 150 people, and I taught over several days. I noticed there was a high level of both satisfaction and involvement of the people in church life and ministry. The pastor explained that his primary focus was that every believer had a 'fivefold' ministry, not in the sense of being appointed as leaders of the church, but in terms of the basic gifting of their lives from which they ministered to the world around them – that they were all gifted with at least one of the gifts of pastoring, prophecy, teaching, soul-winning or leadership, etc. Of course this is a great truth, rarely emphasized, and it was highly motivating in that church. Then the pastor asked me if I would attend his leadership meeting on the Monday night, and spend time with his leadership team.

When I arrived I found about 30 leaders in attendance. They were one of the happiest, most relaxed and at-peace-with-each-other groups I have met. I asked him the secret, and he said that he never gave anyone titles. No-one was called an elder or a deacon, they were simply given leadership roles and all worked together. He said the reason he felt they were integrated and happy, and had a good team spirit, was because these titles were NOT given.

I thought about that often and long; but the real sense of just *why* it was so clicked into place for me later, on the day of the following:

Formative Experience #3 – I 'saw' the 'new' Eldership

I was in Brisbane again, but this time in the South, and I spent one Wednesday teaching a group of about 30 intercessors along with a number of pastors who had gathered for a training day. The year was 2001.

A number of remarkable things happened during the day, but the one I pondered most was this: during the afternoon whilst preaching about the burden of prayer for the city, I suddenly saw what I knew was to be the new eldership.

And it was everything that it was meant to be: biblical, and precisely as defined by the New Testament Scriptures. Suddenly I could see why the old eldership we had entertained all along was not really the New Testament structure of Christianity.

The new eldership was to be a *city* eldership, not a *congregational* eldership. That is, biblical eldership was never something applied in the New Testament to any and every small group that meets as a congregation. In the New Testament it was only ever a single group of people who watched over the whole church of the whole city, town, or region.

And these elders were not drawn from congregational membership. They were identified from amongst the most senior, mature, and trustworthy fivefold ministers of the city. These became a unity, the inspired leadership and the spiritual covering with authority for the blessing and protection of the Body of Christ of the *whole* city.

Of course the local church needs a dynamic leadership team

too. It is of supreme importance that in every congregation we have faithful, believing men and women who stand as one with their senior pastor and other ministers. This is key to making a local church great, and to establishing a greater grace in the life of that congregation. I am so thankful for, and love and appreciate deeply, those who have laboured with me in local churches in every place I have been.

But often, in many places, an 'eldership' operating at the congregational level has been lifeless, or just as often resisted the change that Christ and His ministers would, from time to time, want to bring. At best, it is a trusted group of mature, responsible leaders working for the good of their church and helping their pastor build, lead, and watch over it. This leadership is so valuable, so much needed everywhere, and a vital component to the strength of the local church. Yet this is not the eldership spoken of in the New Testament, nor does it carry anything like the more extensive authority and potential city impact of actual eldership.

It was only two weeks ago whilst visiting a church in a regional town that another visitor, a Presbyterian minister, a wonderful, mature, Godly man, highly respected and an inspiring leader, commented to me how their "system just didn't work." His observation was that mostly their 'elders' didn't "eld." His approach had been to go around trying to motivate them to do some real "elding."

But when, as mentioned above, I suddenly 'saw' that eldership is not congregational, but a group providing the highest level of Christian leadership and covering for the whole city, and always drawn from amongst the ministers of Christ, I understood why it is that so often the local elderships were lacking life, and many were even hindering the progress of the church.

And I understood why not giving titles such as elder and deacon in a local congregation would leave a people in a better and happier state.

CHAPTER FOUR

The Right Elders

"The saying is trustworthy:
If anyone aspires to the office of overseer, he desires a noble task."
(1 Timothy 3:1 ESV)

On a recent Sunday morning I asked my church this question: "What one thing, more than any other, if we prayed for it and saw it come about, would do more to improve our lives, and lift up family life, and bless and protect this church and every church in the city?" The answer was: City Eldership.

The qualifications for church elders laid out by the apostle Paul are found in 1 Timothy 3:1-7 and Titus 1:5-9. In the denominational era of the last five centuries, in a church world in which the Body of Christ has been largely disintegrated in institutional segments, church leaders assumed that the biblical reference to elders *"in every town"*[1] meant that, no matter how small the congregation, elders were to be drawn from the best of the available members of the congregation.

Thus it was that we applied the specifics of Paul's instructions in that context, i.e. within the life of the congregation. And in that way, fishing from that pool, we ended up with good people – doctors, teachers, businessmen, farmers, and the like, serving as congregational elders and then seen as the spiritual leaders of that church along with the ordained minister/s.

---

[1] Titus 1:5

But the truth is, these Scriptural guidelines for appointing elders were meant to be applied to those who had already been raised by the Lord to the fivefold ministry. And the place where we find a 'pool' of these ministers is not in any single congregation, but across all the Body of Christ of the town or region. This is where we can and do happen to find a whole variety of called and appointed ministers of Christ, who have been recognized for their calling and set apart for that purpose. And it is to these, the ministers of the churches, that the qualifications set out by Paul are to be applied when appointing elders.

The apostle makes a statement as strong and specific as needed to clarify this. He tells us that *"in the church God has appointed first of all apostles, second prophets, third teachers, then workers of miracles, also those having gifts of healing, those able to help others, those with gifts of administration, and those speaking in different kinds of tongues"* (1 Corinthians 12:28).

Some immediate observations are these: firstly, where Paul says *"teachers"* we probably should read 'pastor-teachers;' secondly, it is apparent that elders are not drawn from evangelists, since Paul has applied a numerical value indicating priority to only these three, excluded all other gifts and callings in the church from any priority numbering, and then continues his teaching with more generic expressions; and thirdly, if you need to decide who the most senior leaders are, or should be, of the Body of Christ anywhere, why would you bypass the Scripture that says God has appointed first apostles, second prophets, and third teachers?

In any case, the ability to teach and to understand the doctrines of the faith was a requirement of anyone appointed as an elder. Paul instructed Timothy that anyone considered for the eldership must be *"able to teach"* (1 Tim 3:2). Then he expanded instruction on this requirement when writing to Titus, *"He must hold firmly to the trustworthy message as it has been taught, so that he can encourage others by sound doctrine and refute those who oppose it"* (Titus 1:9). Teaching as part of a ministry is, then, a requirement for qualification to the eldership. This alone invalidates most of what has been considered 'eldership' in the past.

Thus the fivefold ministry is where your elders must be found, but with this proviso: not every apostle, not every prophet, not every pastor/teacher, is qualified to be an elder. Notice the inclusion of apostles in that caution.

For those not familiar with the use of apostolic terminology as applied to today's church, see my first book, *The Apostolic Revelation.* Not everyone might like the use of this terminology, but you do need to understand it, and be willing to use it in the way the New Testament does.

When we fail to put eldership into its correct setting, that of being the overall leadership of the Church as the Body of Christ in a given area, we fail – we fail to establish an eldership at all. But that is only the first of our failures.

Yes, we end up with a group in each congregation that is *called* an eldership, but it isn't an eldership. We take good men, good Christian men, who have the Holy Spirit and faith and grace, and we lay hands on them and appoint them as elders, and call them elders, and assume they now have the spiritual authority and grace to be elders. But they are not elders. And when we do this, we obfuscate and hinder the work of the Spirit of Christ in the church.

How so? Because elders, to achieve what eldership is meant to achieve, are to be drawn from those who have the Christ anointing for the fivefold ministry, *in addition* to having exceptional character as men and outstanding maturity as Christian leaders.

This fivefold anointing that every elder must have is crucial.

This is the grace given by Christ to those who are to represent Him in leadership of the Body, and this imparted grace is meant to give a specific outcome – which it does for those who walk in it, pursue the Lord, and lay down their lives in service to the brethren as Christ's servants. It is the God-given sense by which each one is enabled to see the church as Jesus sees it, and to feel about the church as Jesus feels about it. This is an essential endowment of the Spirit, and foundational to genuine city eldership.

Such elders will have a sense of what the Lord wants to do with and for His people (but usually in a growing, progressive fashion that leaves room for search and enquiry, requires waiting on the Lord and listening, and gives growing convictions and sudden insights, and the like). This includes the vision to lead the church and the city where it needs to go spiritually, and includes the grace and the vision to bring change, ensure progress, and confront challenges.

We need to free ourselves from the old denominational picture of an eldership within each denominational congregation. Very often, they became bound with religious tradition, and were intransigent and resistant to the Holy Spirit and their pastor's attempts to lead the church somewhere better. Do you understand why? Because if you take really good people from your congregation who are not called to the ministry, and have no fivefold anointing, but lay hands on them and declare them elders, something quietly and progressively can, and often does, go badly wrong. This is because when we lay hands on unqualified men – unqualified not in *character* but in *calling* – we declare them to have an authority they do not have. We place them in a position to which they do not belong, and for which they are not anointed, and this exposes both them and the church to grave dangers.

The danger to them is that they, over time, without awareness of it, can become proud, religious, and hardened, and actually lock the church up spiritually. But I have also known of cases where good men, truly wonderful brothers who were great servants in the church, became sick and died within a year or two of having a false authority placed on them which, as well-intended as it had been, exposed them to something destructive in the spirit realm – because they did not have the anointing that would protect them in that position. So, some become targets for the devil in one way, and some in another. Presumed authority was placed on them – and it can harm.

For the church the dangers are greater. Such false elderships, even when we have appointed sincere, genuine, mature believers, begin to believe and walk in false assumptions. The chief of these is that, since they are 'the elders,' they believe they are therefore responsible for the protection of the church, and they become wary. They think their role is to guard the church, but if they do not have the essential fivefold anointing, they will lack an important grace. They end up 'protecting' the church, but protecting it from change – and change is precisely what Jesus Christ through the Holy Spirit wants to bring. But the one person who is the most qualified and anointed to lead the church is the pastor, and he's the one trying to bring the change! So it is that, too often, the person who has the greatest grace to perceive the change called for by the Lord, and who seeks to lead the church into this fresh boldness in faith, is the pastor, but he is resisted by the 'eldership.' This will be so if you have the wrong elders.

Now you are aware of one of the primary reasons why numbers of pastors live frustrated lives with elderships; and now you know why, in some places, young people think the elders are never going anywhere. These common problems have occurred because, in completely misconceiving what the eldership is, we laid hands on the wrong people.

So we find there are *two* ways in which the old eldership is 'out of order' (in the sense of not working) – we have had the wrong structure, and we have placed the role on the wrong leaders. But unless we see that eldership is regional, must be drawn from the existing fivefold ministry, and become the senior leaders of the Church in a given area, we do not begin to take hold of what turns out to be, as we will see, an amazing provision of grace and power for the church in the world.

Rather than think that we can draw elders from congregational life, we must come to see that elders are actually found amongst those who have been appointed as fivefold ministers by Christ, AND who are also qualified biblically to be elders. But then, to actually have an effectively functioning eldership, they will need to be appointed in a Godly way to fulfill the very responsible role of being the spiritually authoritative leaders watching over the well-being of the whole of the ministry of Christ in any given community.

In looking for the elders of the future, then, it should be to the pastors, teachers, prophets, and apostles of any given region that we look. It is concerning *them* that the values and character standards given by St. Paul for elders are to be considered as crucial. And the questions that need to be satisfied will be ones that ask about the spirit of their home life, the quality of their marriage relationship, the outcomes in raising their children, what their reputation is in the broader church and community, and so on. We'll see in a moment why this is so vitally important.

Note that in neither version of this list of qualifications supplied by Paul do we find anything that has much to do with what we normally think of as qualifications for the ministry. Yes, in writing to Timothy he lists *"able to teach,"*[2] and instructs Titus that whomever he selects must *"hold firmly"* to what he *"has been taught"* and *"encourage others by sound doctrine,"*[3] but almost entirely the burden of Paul's instructions for choosing elders have to do with character, with requirements covering marriage, morality, family, finance, self-control, honesty, hospitality, holiness, discipline, and more!

2 1 Timothy 3:2
3 Titus 1:9

There are matters of great import attached to this. The eldership has spiritual power and authority to protect the city, just as a pastor does to guard the congregation, and as a husband and father has to protect his own home, wife, and family. These power dynamics are little understood by many, but they are nevertheless real and meant to be used.

At this point, take a moment to read through the instructions given by the apostle:

1 Timothy 3:1-7

(1) Here is a trustworthy saying: If anyone sets his heart on being an overseer, he desires a noble task. (2) Now the overseer must be above reproach, the husband of but one wife, temperate, self-controlled, respectable, hospitable, able to teach, (3) not given to drunkenness, not violent but gentle, not quarrelsome, not a lover of money. (4) He must manage his own family well and see that his children obey him with proper respect. (5) (If anyone does not know how to manage his own family, how can he take care of God's church?) (6) He must not be a recent convert, or he may become conceited and fall under the same judgment as the devil. (7) He must also have a good reputation with outsiders, so that he will not fall into disgrace and into the devil's trap.

Titus 1:5-9

(5) The reason I left you in Crete was that you might straighten out what was left unfinished and appoint elders in every town, as I directed you. (6) An elder must be blameless, the husband of but one wife, a man whose children believe and are not open to the charge of being wild and disobedient. (7) Since an overseer is entrusted with God's work, he must be blameless—not overbearing, not quick-tempered, not given to drunkenness, not violent, not pursuing dishonest gain. (8) Rather he must be hospitable, one who loves what is good, who is self-controlled, upright, holy and disciplined. (9) He must hold firmly to the trustworthy message as it has been taught, so that he can encourage others by sound doctrine and refute those who oppose it.

But, you might think, ought not these qualities be exemplary in every Christian leader, and become so in every faith-filled home. Yes, but the whole reason for such family and character qualifications being highly essential for the eldership specifically, is that if a fivefold minister has not been able to keep divorce, adultery, pornography, addiction, and rebellion etc. out of his own life, or his own home, he ought not, as a general rule, be put in this place of eldership. I'll explain the why of this more in a moment, but first note that the apostle Paul makes of this a most emphatic point – *"If anyone does not know how to manage his own family, how can he take care of God's church?"*[4]

Can he be in the fivefold ministry at all, then? Yes, someone with past sin, mistakes or failure can be in the fivefold ministry. If someone has fallen, then after discipline, heart-felt repentance, and healing – and with humility – they can be restored to serve in whatever way they are now called. Such a person could serve again, having learned serious lessons, being broken and humble, and now wise and mature and willing to carry the burden for others. He could be fully restored to wholeness, holiness, and loving obedience towards God, and be able to pastorally care for people – but don't make him an *elder* of the city.

To understand the importance of this stricture, we have to become familiar with the purpose and authority of the eldership. Simply put, the elders are the gates of the city and the door to the church. Great spiritual authority in and over the city is held and can be used effectively by a real eldership. Such an eldership has great power in their agreement, their prayers, and their word. But whatever comes in or out of their lives, good or evil, both individually and collectively, comes in and out of the city – and the church. This is why an eldership must be made up of those who have not compromised in life, and who have proven themselves to be stable and unlikely to fall or entertain secret sin.

Let me give two examples of the kind of authority I am speaking of, except that in these cases there was no established eldership to turn to; it was a case of someone with apostolic authority agreeing in prayer with a pastor in need.

Some years ago, a young and brash church leader from

---

4 1 Timothy 3:5

South East Queensland started making great claims about himself as an apostle, and started visiting Rockhampton to proclaim his great authority over the whole church of the city. He was deceived, having been buttered up by a false prophet we knew of. They gained the use of one of the local churches on a Saturday night for a meeting they promoted. The spirit of it was not good, and he made all kinds of claims over the pastors of the city, declaring publicly the Lord wanted them to obey him, because he had been given the key for the revival of the city. Frankly, it was all nonsense, but he was dangerous because he was gathering impressionable people and fully intended to make constant repeat visits and to pray and prophesy his claims over the city.

The pastor of the local church whose building they were using came to see me, because he did not know what to make of it all, nor what to do about it. I said, "We can put an end to this right now." I understood how to exercise authority in Christ, and so I shut the gates of the city to the interloper in the spirit realm, gave commands to the unclean spirits that manipulated him, declared that this brother was not an apostle, and that he was not to return. I refused permission, in the Holy Spirit, for him to have spiritual access to the city, and we never saw him again.

The second example occurred in the USA. I was in the Midwest a few years ago as a guest speaker visiting a church I had known for years. It was a well-founded church with a wonderful school. While I was there the pastor shared a very great problem they were going through. They had dismissed a teacher from the school staff who had given them serious problems in school life. They terminated her employment appropriately, but she went on to concoct extensive accusations about the school and its leaders, and took her allegations to high levels of government, involving both educational and judicial officials. There was then being raised against them threatening circumstances and the most serious of enquiries into the administration of that school. The pastor asked me for advice and prayer. I said to him, "You can kill this off right here. This does not have to go any further." I prayed with him, specifically took authority over the principalities and powers that were driving this woman, and refused them permission to pursue this any longer. I cut off the lies and accusations, bound the spirits, broke the witchcraft, and refused permission in the spirit realm by the name of Jesus for this matter to go any further. I released the pastor, the church, and the school from the accusations, and declared that none of this was allowed to come against them. At that point the matter was totally finished, nothing further came of it, they were left completely in peace, and their accuser stopped pursuing them.

These are Godly outcomes from the use of apostolic authority. It will be found that authority similar to this is vested in elderships. That is one reason why these should be *"in every town."* Then the Body of Christ everywhere would have much higher levels of protection, blessing, power, authority, and peace. And besides, the eldership is the key to the Body of Christ becoming of one heart and one mind. And that is the proper state of the church.

But understanding who the right elders are, and what they are meant to achieve for the church, is only the first step. Establishing in the hearts of the whole church and all fivefold leaders a right understanding concerning how elders are meant to *think* and *act* towards each other is the greater challenge. It is a matter of having not only the right people as elders, but of them also having a right spirit. That is necessary if we are to have the right eldership.

And that brings us to a matter of great moment:

An Even *Greater* Biblical Qualification for Eldership

Without doubt the single most important qualification for elders is this: that they **love**, not just 'everybody' in a general sense, but *each other* from the heart.

Paul wrote chapter 13 of First Corinthians for all believers, in which he taught, *"If I... have not love, I am nothing,"* and *"...the greatest of these is love."* If these truths are to be taken seriously by every believer and for the whole church, it must apply in the first instance to the church's most senior spiritual leaders.

And there is much else in Scripture that labours this point, including the most serious of all the instructions given by Christ as well as the apostles and others who were used by the Holy Spirit to write the inspired canon.

Consider the import of the following examples – but as you read them, think of these as being written about the relationships and heart attitudes of Christ's most senior leaders, the 'apostles and elders,' a phase used repeatedly in Acts 15 to describe the apostles, prophets, and teachers who had gathered for the Jerusalem Council.

Christ gave His instructions in the first instance to His apostles, not as preaching points they could use in ministry, but as commands about how they were meant to live in relationship with each other. And if this is of the highest order for the apostles, how is it that any minister of the gospel anywhere can think it does not apply to his or her relationships with the other fivefold ministers – not those afar, but *right in the town where they live*!

Jesus' Commands–

> *'Jesus called the Twelve and said, "If anyone wants to be first, he must be the very last, and the servant of all."'* (Mark 9:35)

> *"you... should wash one another's feet. I have set you an example that you should do as I have done for you."* (John 13:14-15)

Paul's Command –

> *"Be devoted to one another in brotherly love. Honor one another above yourselves."* (Romans 12:10)

Paul's Angst –

> *"...since there is jealousy and quarreling among you, are you not worldly? Are you not acting like mere men? For when one says, "I follow Paul," and another, "I follow Apollos," are you not mere men?"* (1 Corinthians 3:3-4)

Peter's Observation and Command –

> *"... you have purified yourselves by obeying the truth so that you have sincere love for your brothers.... Now... love one another deeply, from the heart."* (1 Peter 1:22 – rearranged for clarity)

John's Heart Cry –

> *"Whoever loves his brother lives in the light..."* (1 John 2:10)

> *"... if we walk in the light, as he is in the light, we have fellowship with one another..."* (1 John 1:7)

> *"if we love one another, God lives in us..."* (1 John 4:12)

> *"Jesus Christ laid down his life for us. And we ought to lay down our lives for our brothers."* (1 John 3:16)

A Complaint

I have a complaint to express against many pastors of all denominations, and those that are in none, and at all levels of leadership, but especially the most senior. Many have made a big mistake, and are in error.

What is this error? Let me speak directly to those to whom this might apply. In your charge over the congregation, you have taught many things in righteousness, including the need to be one, to love one another, to be of one heart, to work together, that you are members of one another, that you must look out for the weak especially the weaker brother, that you must honour one another more than yourself, and accept one another as Christ has accepted you. And you've supplied chapter and verse. And you know that this is Christianity – that to love, accept, honour, and live for others like this, and to lay down your lives for the brethren, is to follow Christ and to be Christlike!

And if in your congregation there were pockets of exclusiveness, and superior attitudes towards other members, and judgement and criticism of others, or jealousy in the flock, or disdain felt by some families towards other families, you would be deeply burdened, and pray and preach and work to clean it out of the body of your congregation. There would be no freedom from the burden of concern 'til you had done so, and great relief and gladness when it was achieved.

You have applied these Christian spiritual values and all this valuable truth to the congregation, and pleaded for change, but you have not applied it to yourself. Do you not realise, *these truths apply in the first instance to the ministers of the Body of Christ in their relations with one another.*

In this matter, too many have been like the blind leading the blind.

Why is it that we see this as great truth that we strive to perfect at the congregational level, but ignore completely at the city-wide level, when in fact that is what the church is. Jesus walks among the lampstands, which are the churches, but for any given city, there is only one lampstand. A multi-branch lampstand was the image, to be sure, but of one whole. There is no other kind of Body.

And Paul declares: *"There is one body and one Spirit–just as you were called to one hope when you were called– one Lord, one faith, one baptism; one God and Father of all, who is over all and through all and in all"* (Ephesians 4:4-6).

Why is it then that the church as a whole is so disparate? Light on that subject will be shed more in a later chapter of this book, but for now, consider our basic problem. The following scenario has exceptions, but is otherwise typical of towns and cities everywhere:

> Across our towns and cities, the ministers know each other hardly at all, and there are very few genuine and personal friendships. When they do meet, it is usually to attend a brief 'business' meeting that may be regular but not that frequent, it doesn't last long, and the pastors are mostly closed and careful with each other, not saying too much. There is very little thought put into building deeper and long-lasting friendships, let alone the need to build the city's ministers together as brothers deep in love, knowing each other intimately, and trusting each other as one, from the heart. And if the need to 'work more closely together' is mentioned by someone, it will receive assent from everyone present, but nothing is done about it and nothing ever changes.

But New Testament Eldership is Not Like That

The New Testament eldership we must have is different from the posturing, private, independent, cards-close-to-your-chest politicking, arms-length positioning, only-commit-to-your-own-denominational-vested-interest, always-too-busy-in-our-own-parish kind of fivefold leadership.

Consider the following:

- True elders of the original kind become the great fathers of the city; this is a multiplicity of shepherds, a team of those with the most trusted and trustworthy spiritual maturity, always drawn from the fivefold ministry – but there is more! As said above, the single most important qualification for the eldership is this: they must **love**, not just 'everyone' but specifically ***each*** *other*, from the heart.

- Not only so, but there is an adjoining grace that is just as important and must be evident: this is the humility by which any one of them is willing for someone else to serve in their place. There can be no grasping control.

- This eldership does not 'own' the church: they won't own the real estate or control the money, nor run every local program or hold the vision for what every individual ministry will do.

- Valuing openness and honesty with each other, understanding accountability to the others and freely walking in it, and each with a spirit of submission and of the holy fear of the Lord, they will *"submit to one another out of reverence for Christ"⁵* in all humility. They are here for each other as well as the church. They seek not their own advancement, but the success of others. They look to build the whole Body, and protect the whole Body, and to advance the cause and Kingdom of our Lord Jesus Christ. Too many have done otherwise, but not the *right* elders. (Paul, in a much more difficult time than our own, made this observation, *"... everyone looks out for his own interests, not those of Jesus Christ. But you know that Timothy has proved himself...,"⁶* but we are better placed in this day, with many faithful like Timothy everywhere. We can learn better the ways of God, and walk in them. All over the world, the Holy Spirit will build these elderships as we allow Him.)

- The right elders will see themselves as called to be long-term servants to the city, with a heart devoted to the city and the whole Body. They will have a vision for the city, and for the direction of church life in the city as a whole.

- Not only so, but they will have a heart for *all* the ministers and congregations, for Christian schools as well, and all the missions and outreaches based in the city, and will watch over them all with prayer, and guard the hearts and lives of the

5 Ephesians 5:21
6 Philippians 2:21-22

ministers of Christ. Because theirs is not a sectarian interest, they do not function out of a denominational mindset, nor operate only to the building up of their own ministry. They are there for the whole, not the part. They have left behind the false love of vested interest. They have found the way of Christ.

- Theirs is a spiritual watch, and when such an eldership is anointed, and maintained in love and unity, it has great authority and genuine spiritual power. Theirs is authority not only to love and build up, but also to correct and discipline ministers and groups, and to stand for the sound doctrine of the church.[7]

- It is their prerogative, too, to stand against anything in the community, or that seeks to come into the community, that is godless. This includes all things spiritual, natural, religious, political, moral, financial, industrial, and includes sport and entertainment. The eldership has great power to refuse permission, in the spirit realm, to anything that ought not come into the city. They have authority to judge such things.[8]

- And the right eldership caringly and prayerfully watches over the spiritual life of the church, and stands to protect God's people and help keep them from false loves, mediocrity, and every scheme of the devil. But all this grace and power is rooted in their love for one another. Spiritually, they are close as brothers, and they are fathers and sons to others. They are most relational, and all use of authority is understood and expressed relationally, just like a good dad would do in a family home. By thinking about the family home, we can more easily envisage what is intended here – genuine authority and leadership is in place, but flows through great fathering love, and is always seeking the good of all others in the family.

A *Relational* Understanding of Christian Leadership

At this point I must say again, it is essential that we all come to understand the Body of Christ from a relational point of view, not an institutional one. Christianity *is* relationships, relationships, relationships!!

7 Titus 1:9
8 1 Corinthians 2:15, 5:3, 6:1, 7:25, 11:31

Church leadership, at every level, if it is to be apostolic in nature and therefore properly of the faith, is not controlling, hierarchical, or authoritarian – it is deeply relational, yet with genuine authority in Christ. Only insight given by the Holy Spirit can, in the end, make this more understood to the reader, because spiritual truth is spiritually discerned. Without grace to understand, we will always think in natural terms and end up operating religiously. This is because, without our eyes being *"enlightened,"*[9] we think like *"mere men."*[10] This is what Paul remonstrated with the Corinthians over.[11] We must make this journey into proper relational Christianity; it is a priority of the highest order.

Now the apostle Peter said he was *"a fellow elder."*[12] Imagine for a moment what it might be like if we had people in our city who *in their hearts* were like the apostle Peter, or like John or Paul – who had that kind of love, that kind of heart for the Lord and the church, with tenderness and gentleness, having authority from the Lord, and who would take a stand when they had to take a stand. And imagine that these are not strangers to the church, not Christians we know of at a distance and never feel close to.

Here is the point: we can have such fathers for our cities!

And we already have around us, in most every place, an abundance of ministers who have all this potential, because they do love both God and His people, and they do have great hearts; but they have labored under restraints that have been imposed upon the church as a whole by entrenched religious ways of thinking and traditions that keep the bulk of people locked into small-mindedness. It is mostly a denominational blindness. But now we come to better days, and should believe, for it is Christ who gives the grace for such things. Even being able to envisage and speak of these things with some clarity is because grace has been given. So by that we can be assured that we are seeing the ongoing maturing of the church, and

9 Ephesians 1:18
10 1 Corinthians 3:4
11 1 Corinthians 1:10-13, 3:1-4, 4:6, 4:14-21.
12 1 Peter 5:1

Christ will provide and raise up elderships.

I sought to explain above that a team of leaders like this, built together in intimate trusting relationships, has tremendous spiritual authority to decide what should, and what should not, come into the city. The elders are the spiritual guardians of the city.

To help us understand this, think of the walled cities spoken of in the time of Old Testament Israel. And think of Nehemiah rebuilding the walls and re-hanging the gates of Jerusalem. These were real walls and gates to keep out enemies and secure the city, but they are used in the Bible as powerful symbols of spiritual realities. For instance, Isaiah prophesied that we will call our walls Salvation, and our gates Praise.[13] John, in speaking of the New Jerusalem, said the angel who spoke with him had a measuring rod to measure the city and its gates and walls.[14] This is all symbolism of the church and the spiritual realities associated with its life and the gospel. The Psalmist interceded, *"In your good pleasure make Zion prosper; build up the walls of Jerusalem"* (Psalm 51:18), a reference to the spiritual wellbeing, progress, blessing, and security of God's people in every age.

The church in every place is meant to build up spiritual walls for their people, the city of God. These walls, called Salvation, are built by the unity of the church and the intercession of the saints. But the *gates* of the city of God, the church, are the *elders* of the church of the city. These are they who guard the city – and have authority to close the gates against evil.

In the old walled cities, by day the elders sat in the gates judging the affairs of the community and witnessing and approving business transactions and the like. At night, those gates were shut, locked, and guarded. If someone arrived outside wanting access, the watchman could not open a gate to allow entry without getting the approval of an elder to do so.

---

13 Isaiah 60:18
14 Revelation 21:15

But we have a problem. As it was in Nehemiah's day that caused him to mourn, so it is in our cities: our walls are down, and our gates have been burned.[15] So everything and anything comes in; pornography, homosexuality, divorce, and adultery become rampant. Drugs and addiction, violence and crime. Marriages break down, and children more and more are raised in single-parent families. And love of the world has too much hold on the church - because we are lacking one of the most significant and vital components of church life that the Lord appointed for us.

Nehemiah acted, and so must we. *'(He) said to them, "You see the trouble we are in: Jerusalem lies in ruins, and its gates have been burned with fire. Come, let us rebuild the wall of Jerusalem, and we will no longer be in disgrace" '* (Nehemiah 2:17).

For the obvious question, "Who then guards the eldership?" there is a biblical answer. That we will consider later in the book.[16]

For now we need to see that if we want spiritual change so as to achieve a better kind of spiritual life for our people and our cities, then we need to see restored the full biblical function of New Testament eldership.

Earlier I pleaded the case, on the basis of Paul's instructions, for only allowing those mature fivefold ministers who have never fallen, and do not have weaknesses that might lead to sin, to be placed in the eldership. You might ask, can there be exceptions? My answer might be, "Perhaps, but at your peril! Elders are the Gates of the City." I know the Holy Spirit can make exceptions to the rule if He so desires – He is the all-wise, all-knowing God – but you make exceptions to the rule at your peril, because the elders guard the city.

---

15 Nehemiah 1:3
16 In Chapter 8

CHAPTER FIVE

Denominational Principalities

The Infiltration of Christian Institutions by Powers of Darkness

'He presented another parable to them, saying,
"The kingdom of heaven is like a mustard seed, which a man took
and sowed in his field;
and this is smaller than all other seeds, but when it is full grown,
it is larger than the garden plants and becomes a tree, so that
the birds of the air come and nest in its branches." '
(Matthew 13:31-32 NASB)

I began this book by saying, "On Sunday, December 3, 2006... I preached a message relative to the spiritual state of denominations and Christian institutions... I called it *'The State of the War.'* " And I advised that on the evening of the same day, as instructed by the Lord, I drove around and prayed a simple prayer for each of the churches in the city, after which, during an extensive drought period, the rains were released over the city.

I must first explain the substance of that message, after which I can answer the question, re-stated here, that I posed in Chapter One:

What kind of prayer, so brief as to take a mere 30 seconds, repeated over each of the denominations and independent churches as well as our own, could bring this kind of dramatic outcome – and in the one thing that is the biblical sign of an open or closed heaven?

And may I remind us all of St. Paul's clarity on this point: *"…our struggle is… against the rulers, against the authorities, against the powers of this dark world and against the spiritual forces of evil in the heavenly realms"* (Ephesians 6:12).

I caution the reader of the need to be wise in considering the things I am about to raise, and to see things in their larger perspective, as there is a danger of false conclusions. The information I am about to divulge, learned over many years of prayer, pastoral leadership, and mission, has been very useful to my wife and I. It proved to be a powerfully effective insight for use in spiritual warfare prayer and overcoming dark powers. But I always thought I could not make this information a public matter because it would be too easy for some to misunderstand, and for the weak in faith to make an abusive use of it. But on the Sunday in question, I was instructed by the Lord to do the thing I was wary of, and to teach it publicly. I am happy to report there were no negative consequences, but rather an increase of faith and freedom in the congregation.

The *Corporate* Struggle with Demonic Power

What we must look at is the very real issue of the alarming extent to which demonic power is actively involved and interfering with, not just individuals in their spiritual struggles, but the corporate life and struggle of the Body of Christ – in denominations, in Christian institutions in general, and in the life of cities too.

In the late nineties, while preparing for one of our annual conferences, I decided to spend a whole night in prayer and waiting on God. For most of the night I was not conscious of the Lord showing me anything, but as I continued praying and listening, at about 4.00 a.m. there opened to me a clear insight into something that goes on in the spirit realm relative to all denominations – but not only denominations, it occurs in all the institutions of Christianity, including the very small ones, i.e. independent churches.

Parable of the Mustard Seed

I was led to the Scripture passage quoted at the head of this chapter, Mark 4:30-32: *"Again he said, 'What shall we say the kingdom of God is like, or what parable shall we use to describe it? It is like a mustard seed, which is the smallest seed you plant in the ground. Yet when planted, it grows and becomes the largest of all garden plants, with such big branches that the birds of the air can perch in its shade.'"*

This parable, with the same final point, is found in all the synoptic gospels, and the punchline in Matthew 13:32 (NIV84) reads, *"...yet when it grows... the birds of the air come and perch in its branches."* In Luke 13:19 the statement is near identical.

It will become so big, the Lord said, that the *"birds of the air"* will find a place for themselves in it: they will rest in its shade; they will *"perch"* in its *"branches."* What are these 'birds of the air?' And what are these 'branches?' What does it mean to 'perch' in them? It is not too hard to answer these questions.

Of course I wasn't expecting what I was shown. But it all made sense.

In describing what the Kingdom of God on earth would be like, Jesus makes it clear that even though it starts small, it grows to become the largest living organism in the world. And even now, visible Christianity, in all its forms taken together, is already the largest entity on earth. But there in the middle of the night, the Lord made it clear that those *"birds of the air"* are demonic powers.

We must note that the *"birds of the air"* and the *"branches"* are two very different things. Whilst the branches are part of the tree, the birds are not part of the tree, but they find it very accessible and useful to them. The church has put out many branches all over the world, and such birds come and find lodging in their shade. **In other words, there are demonic powers that find the branches of the church a comfortable place in which to take up residence. And every 'branch' will have a battle with these influences.**

The symbols used in the Bible are used with consistency, and when the Holy Spirit uses a particular symbol in the sacred canon, you can reliably interpret the symbol by examining its use throughout the Scriptures. To confirm that the symbol we are here considering, the *"birds of the air,"* does actually represent demonic principalities and powers, at least as far as the parables of Jesus are concerned, we need only go back but a few verses in the same chapter in both Matthew 13 and Mark 4, to another parable told by Jesus, the Parable of the Sower (in Luke it is found in Chapter 8).

In this more familiar parable, in Matthew 4:4 Jesus teaches, *"the birds came and ate it up,'* and the interpretation given by Jesus at v.19 is, *"the evil one comes and snatches away what was sown...,"* and in Mark 4:4, again, *"the birds came and ate it up,'* with the interpretation by Jesus recorded at v.15 as, *"Satan comes and takes away the word that was sown."* So in one gospel, the *"birds of the air"* are *"the evil one"* and in the other gospel they are *"Satan,"* obviously a reference to the same devil. And as if the Holy Spirit wanted to leave no doubt about the intent of the symbol, in Luke's version it is *"the devil"* (Luke 8:12).

We are being consistent then, and allowing Scripture to interpret Scripture, to conclude that Jesus' use of the same figure of speech at the same period of time in His ministry can be emphatically held to speak of the same demonic activity. Except that this time the parable is referring to a corporate outcome, rather than the personal context of the earlier parable.

An Old Testament example is found in Ecclesiastes 10:20, *"Do not revile the king even in your thoughts, or curse the rich in your bedroom, because a **bird of the air** may carry your words,* *and **a bird on the wing** may report what you say."* I quote this only to demonstrate the use of a symbol that has consistentcy in both Old and New Testaments. You may speak in the privacy of your bedroom, but if what you say is slander or gossip or a curse, *"a bird of the air,"* i.e. an evil spirit, picks up on it and carries it as a spirit of witchcraft, as demonic power, which you yourself have 'authorised' by your bitterness, unforgiveness, and sin. Anyway, there is consistency in the use of the figure of speech. (I note, too, there are places in Scripture where birds of the air are referred to without this being a figure of speech.)

Parable of the Yeast

There is another small parable in Matthew 13:33. In this one verse Jesus said, *"The kingdom of God is like yeast that a woman took and mixed into about sixty pounds of flour until it worked all through the dough."* This verse from the NIV version unfortunately doesn't really tell us exactly what Jesus said. In the original Greek text Jesus was very particular in saying it was three (3) measures (Gk. *three satas*) of flour. The translators didn't see anything significant about the use of the word "three" so they left it out, translating it into a modern equivalent volume amount. However, the "three" needs to go back in if we are to understand Jesus' message.

The parable, describing what will happen in the Kingdom of Heaven, is telling us it will be like a woman taking yeast and working or kneading it all through the dough. We need to interpret the symbols here. Biblically yeast always represents evil or sin, and the dough or the lump that is to become bread represents the church or God's people.

The fact that there were "three" measures of meal or flour is symbolic of divinity. "Three" is symbolic of God the Father, God the Son, and God the Holy Spirit. The meal is the pure meal of God's Word. Who then is the woman?

The woman is the Church. Whenever we come across a

woman in a parable, or in the life of Jesus, such as the healing of the Canaanite woman's daughter, or meeting the woman at the well, that woman is symbolic of the Church in some way. So here we have a tiny parable packed with meaning.

Jesus is telling us that something is going to go on in the church. The woman, i.e. the church, is going to take leaven, which is always symbolic of sin or evil, and mix it into the three measures of meal, that is into the divine truth of God's Word, until the whole lump is leavened – a mixture. Welcome to reality. Welcome to the world in which we live!

God has given us a divine revelation of truth in the Scriptures and in Jesus Christ. He has given us the apostles and the prophets, He's given us our Saviour and the gospel, and He's given us the Word of God and the Holy Spirit by which we may understand divine truth – but the Church of the centuries has continually mixed leaven into the dough until we find that in churches everywhere there is this leaven at work. It is a mixture, of truth and error, of righteousness and flesh, of freedom and bondage, of being awake and asleep, of life and dead tradition.

Denominational Backgrounds

The truth is, all of us were brought up in circumstances where we were taught much that was true, but some that was not. Many of us were raised in denominational backgrounds or family circumstances in which we were given a certain way of seeing the world. This worldview directly affects the way we appraise the world around us, it gives us a framework for the way we live and think. In all that, with a Christian denominational background, there will be good and helpful things to live by, but there is also mixture.

A lot of the bondage in people's lives comes from religious ideas that are not actually quite the truth. The Lord establishes good in the earth, but the enemy seeks to infiltrate it. This is where the *"birds of the air"* come and seek to roost in the branches of the Kingdom of God. And besides, the flesh of man provides open doors even into the highest levels of leadership. In churches and amongst church leaders everywhere you will find instances of selfish ambition, slander, criticism, judgemental assumptions, lust, secret sin, control, and a big one, jealousy. Not to mention pride and superiority, just as dangerous. We could name other things which, as you know, are common to fallen man, and you also know are too often found at senior church leadership levels. Any one of these things yields access and potential control of the church in any place, including its denominations, to demonic powers.

Do you think it doesn't? Then let James, the great pastoral leader of the New Testament church in Jerusalem, disagree with you: *"But if you harbor bitter envy and selfish ambition in your hearts, do not boast about it or deny the truth. Such "wisdom" does not come down from heaven but is earthly, unspiritual, demonic. For where you have envy and selfish ambition, there you find disorder and every evil practice"* (James 3:14-16).

James' language is very strong. In referencing *"envy"* and *"selfish ambition,"* he says this is not only *"unspiritual,"* but also *"demonic!"* And he says that where these occur, you find *"every evil practice."* This is not just any ordinary error or weakness; James says it is *"evil."* And he is speaking about the church. Don't tell me there is not a strong case for explaining that the institutions of Christianity get infiltrated by demonic powers. They do, and they have.

We need to acknowledge that in the two thousand year history of the church the enemy has always sought to mix leaven into its many branches, and this has been done often through well-meaning, but religious people. I would argue, then, that demonic principalities and powers access the church, seeking to control it, and pulling levers of power, through at least two separate things. One, the sinful flesh, especially of individuals who have responsibility and authority in the church, but also through the religious nature of so much vain tradition that is dead. Tradition and Religion are powerful principalities, and these intelligent powers find the unguarded, religiously naïve church easy prey.

This occurs in all denominations, missionary movements, theological colleges, and institutions of the church. Independent churches too. Thus we find a situation in which, all over the world, Christian denominations have in them good people, and good truths, and good works – I am not denying that a lot of the work is good; as far as I know, much of the work is good – but what we also have in every one of these movements, at the least, is the reality of satanic desire and satanic schemes to build demonic strongholds on the inside. These can then be manipulated, so as to control, hinder, and set aside the work into powerlessness. As Jesus said to the Pharisees, *"You have let go of the commands of God and are holding on to the traditions of men... Thus you nullify the word of God by your tradition that you have handed down"* (Mark 7:8, 13a).

What has happened historically is that new Christian movements start out with a breakthrough; they begin with people who are living holy lives, devoted to the cause of Christ, and who have been seeking God. They obtain grace and find themselves greatly empowered. They have such power that missions and churches everywhere are multiplied, bringing many people to Christ.

But then the movement settles down into their own assumptions, which become, in time, routine and powerless. What were previously exciting new ways of doing things now become the traditions of the organisation, dictating how things are to be done. It is easy enough for a religious spirit to work with that, and harden it, so that within a few generations, or less, the energy of life, if not the light, has gone out of that movement. Usually, within a hundred, years every new movement has long lost its momentum and is becoming ossified, unless dynamically renewed by the Holy Spirit in answer to the earnest prayers of seeking, hungry, obedient believers – and praise God we have had that too!!

There are no doubt many examples of this, but I will quote my own background in the beloved Salvation Army by way of illustration. The Salvation Army has a record as excellent and outstanding as any movement could desire. The story of General William Booth is so exceptional I don't think there is anyone like him in church history; a totally unique servant of Christ, completely yielded to God, leading a Holy Spirit raised movement that was given tremendous power. Booth went from being one evangelist to having ten thousand evangelists under his powerful command in just twenty-five years, and his Salvation Army in that time went to eighty nations and brought millions of thirsty souls to Christ, most of whom had no knowledge of God until the Salvation Army got there.

My maternal great-great-grandfather was a terrible drunkard, an alcoholic, until the Salvation Army arrived in the North of England in the late 1800s. He was one of the first to be profoundly converted to Christ, and all his descendants then lived transformed lives (I have a photo of his son, my great-grandfather, with his five sons, all in Salvation Army uniform with their brass instruments). My wife Hazel's paternal great-great-grandfather was a dreadful drunkard here in Rockhampton in the late 1800s. He was saved in an open-air meeting, kneeling at the bass drum laid on its side, which was what they did, using it as their mercy seat or penitent form when inviting people to Christ in public. From him came generations of Godly descendants, many of them ministers of the gospel.

An early Salvation Army slogan was, "Christ for the World, the World for Christ," and a further Booth instruction to the troops was, "Go for souls, and go for the worst." And in those days the Holy Spirit fell with great power on their prayer meetings, week after week. There are many astonishing stories of what was accomplished during those times.

But William Booth had stated that he had no desire to see the Salvation Army end up like so many other dead religious bodies that littered the landscape of the earth. He said that if ever the power went out of the Army, it would be better to close it down rather than have another ecclesiastical dead body.

What was he recognising? That most of the denominations had encountered this deathly, rigid, religious kind of fossilising in their traditions. For even though they were full of good people who loved the Lord and believed and upheld the truths, little of the life or power was left. Not in all, but in too many.

Of course they did not close the Salvation Army when its strength and freedom faded. You know that to all practical intents and purposes that can't be done, and shouldn't be done. Rather, every generation should seek to renew the life of the Holy Spirit in the work. But many fail to do this. It continued on, and today the Salvation Army is full of good people who have good truths, and who do good works. And still regularly bring, here and there, people to Christ. But they do not have the power they had, and in many ways the movement is bound.

In the early days the Salvation Army found that, in ministering in the slums, one of the most powerful things they could do to attract people to the preaching of the gospel, especially in the culture of the day, was to form brass bands (I spent 25 years of my life playing in Army bands, and I come from a line of Salvation Army bandmasters). This method attracted thousands of people who would gather and then follow the bands back to a meeting where they would yield to Christ and find salvation by grace. There was great, great power in those open-air meetings and in the street preaching of the Army.

A hundred years later, when I grew up in the Salvation Army, we were still doing those same things, but several major changes had taken place in society. For one, television was in every home, with the consequence that the brass band in the street was no longer big entertainment. Yet even though nobody came to listen, except perhaps to carols at Christmas time, there was no great freedom, or strength of will, or official approval, to change the program – nor was there any inspiration as to what to do next. It was religious bondage through which no-one much could see anything.

In Canberra, where Hazel and I were teenagers in the early 70s, we had open-air meetings right in the city on Friday and Sunday evenings. The Friday night event was still relevant; it was late night shopping and we were in a street busy with pedestrians. But the Sunday evening in Garema Place, a concrete quadrangle surrounded by shops that on Sunday were all closed, was another story. In summer the weather was quite pleasant and occasionally people would wander through, but no-one had any great reason for going there on a Sunday, and in winter, by 6.00p.m., which was the starting time for our open-air meeting, it was dark and freezing cold with sometimes a howling wind blowing through! Along with the pigeons, thirty or forty of us would group up, the brass band and the timbrel girls would play, and others sing.

Every Sunday night after the preaching, the Corps Sergeant-Major would make the same announcement, "It's lovely to see all of you listening here tonight, and we invite you to come back to the meeting." But there was no-one there! Not one, solitary person had walked through the whole time. All winter long there never was a soul there, but you couldn't change the program!

But we had done our duty, offered our sacrificial service to the Kingdom of God, and satisfied the statistical report that said we were maintaining the witness of the corps! And in the four years I was there, from December 1969 until March 1974, it never varied. It's an extreme example of one tradition I was personally familiar with, but every other denomination has these and other strange things that go on. It is a religious bondage that keeps us locked in tradition. Again, as Jesus said, *"you nullify the word of God for the sake of your tradition"* (Matthew 15:6).

But it is worse than we think. When we are no longer operating by the power of the Holy Spirit, under the leadership of anointed and inspired Godly leaders, but just maintaining the work, we become easy prey for the elemental spirits of the air. This is just one way in which the *"birds of the air"* come and roost in the branches – and then find their way further in, so as to control and manipulate. Tradition is a very effective way for the enemy, and every religious spirit finds comfort and shade in such churches.

Once unclean spirits gain some power in the house, they begin exerting influence, through people, to change the spirit of the movement, changing the values, the attitudes, even the teaching emphasis.

John Wesley was one of the greatest Christian leaders who ever lived. Two hundred years after Luther, the reformation of the Church was still ongoing, as it is today. The Lord raised Wesley and gave him great understanding of both experiential holiness and the evangelical nature of the gospel. He brought to the world a greater and proper emphasis on what it means to live a holy life in the power of the Holy Spirit, and the public preaching of the gospel with an invitation to respond. Think how much of what we all have has come from that! The Lord used him to take our understanding of spiritual life for both the Church and the believer to another height. Today, every evangelical and Pentecostal church in the world has some of John Wesley's spiritual DNA.

Yet sadly, some of his more direct spiritual descendants are a long way from John Wesley's spirituality, and even struggling over what the Scriptures say is right and wrong for those in the faith. This kind of confusion and mixture, and the tendency to adopt society's values rather than be sold out to the Spirit of Holiness, is the result of a demonic power having come and rested in the branches of the church. And then, in time, even unregenerate men and women find their way into some of the most senior positions of church leadership.

The Background to My Discovery

The church that in 1987 invited me to become their pastor and lead them into renewal was a Baptist church, and a committed part of the denomination. The history of our church went back as far as 1888, with Baptist churches developing over the years in North Rockhampton, Park Avenue, Lakes Creek, and Mount Morgan, which had all, along the way, amalgamated to form Peace Memorial Baptist Church by the early 70s. I began ministry leadership at Peace in January, 1988.

By 1991, we were developing a sense of call to international mission, and by 1993 the apostolic purpose of that mission was becoming clear. The pace picked up, and all through the rest of the 90s I was travelling internationally four or five times a year with a growing and urgent sense of apostolic mission. All the while I was most supportive of the denomination – in fact we had become the most generous of the churches to the denominational budget. I had personally insisted on the principle of our church tithing when I first came to the leadership.

But early in the year 2000 a decision was made by the consensus of the members of the church to resign from the denomination. The belief that this was what we were to do came from many of the members individually, and it was they who proposed it to the leadership as being, they felt, the leading of the Holy Spirit. When the leaders sought the Lord, they came unanimously to that conclusion also. So it was that we separated amicably, and negotiated a property/financial settlement.

It became clear to us what the Lord was saying: that for us to do what He wanted us to do in the world, we had to work from outside the denominational system. After prayer I felt clear about this purpose, and said to the congregation, "We want to be one with the whole Body of Christ." Borrowing sentiment from St Paul, I said, "To the Anglicans, we need to be Anglican, and to the Pentecostals, we need to be Pentecostal."[1]

Over the next two years, our church experienced amazing breakthroughs, the nature of which I explain in my books, *The Spirit of Sonship*, and *Building an Apostolic People* (formerly entitled *Holy Community*).

But on those international mission trips, whether to the Philippines, Cambodia, Malaysia, India, Africa, North America, or Europe, I would very often feel waves of nausea within a day of arriving at my destination. It was never enough to really hinder me, it was often in the background, or would come and go, and I would pray, rebuke and resist it, and get some relief, but I was never sure about the reasons for it. My basic assumption was that probably someone at home was complaining about me being away, and that was activating the spirit of witchcraft. So I would forgive and bless, and keep going.

Sometimes the nausea lasted just a few days, and sometimes it would come and go during the whole trip. In 2001, however, I came home from one of those trips and this time the nausea stayed on and on for days; and this time it was stronger than ever. It had become a heavy burden.

After three days, I said to my wife Hazel, "I'm sick of this. We have to seek the Lord and nail this thing. We have to identify where this is coming from." We were about to receive a big surprise.

We had hardly begun to pray when Hazel said, "I hope I've got this right; I'd hate to say this and be wrong. But I heard the Lord say, 'It's the Baptist spirit.'"

I thought, "What? That couldn't possibly be."

---

1 1 Corinthians 9:20-23

What I couldn't believe, as a first reaction, was that an unclean spirit, a demonic power, could be known by such a *Christian* name – i.e. that it could be named using what I would have thought was such a biblical concept. And it had not occurred to me that there was such a thing as a principality that was basically a territorial spirit, an institutional one, operating from a power base within a church structure. A *denominational* spirit!

An Institutional Religious *Spirit*

I turned to the Lord in prayer again, asking the Lord to show me the truth. Within moments, my eyes were opened to see into the spirit realm, and the Lord showed me what this *Baptist spirit* was. What I saw was a powerful demon, a religious spirit, that had infiltrated the denomination in the course of its history. It manipulated and pulled levers of power, and all over the State of Queensland was powerfully influencing or resisting the life of churches. It had infiltrated many churches as well as Head Office, and was 'controlling' many things that went on. I saw further that it was also manipulating two churches in Rockhampton that were not, in fact, Baptist. It was this spirit that had resisted me all the years I was in the denomination, and though we had left 18 months before, was still opposing us.

Please note: I am not saying that this spirit is the Baptist *Church*, or Baptist *people*, whom I always loved and served and sought to honour. I'm simply reporting there to be a spirit being, an independent, intelligent entity, a high-level demonic power, that is specifically assigned to oppose, control, and manipulate Baptist churches, and others, in our State (and, you will soon see, every institution has the same, or similar, spiritual battle for control going on). This had gained entrance as these things do, and in describing it to us in answer to our prayers, the Lord called it 'the Baptist spirit.'

The proof, they say, is in the pudding. Once I saw what this was, I took authority over the 'Baptist spirit' in the Lord's name, rebuked its opposition to me, and cut it off from pursuing me. Immediately the nausea ceased, and never came back. That was over fifteen years ago.

Sometime later we were in another State visiting a couple that had been in Christian leadership in renewal type churches for many years. At this stage they had their own church with a very effective pastoral care ministry, they were living Godly lives in prayer and walking with God, and putting into practice what they learned. Yet although there was much blessing in their lives, they had over the years been opposed and resisted by something that also manifested in sickness and disease.

Hazel and I went there in faith, hoping to help them find the grace of God for the wife's healing from cancer. We enjoyed dinner with them, and then spent the whole evening in prayer – and in those several hours again found things we were not expecting. It was like taking the layers off an onion, one thing under another.

We peeled the issues back but in the end found at the core the thing we were not expecting. This couple were, in earlier years, very well-known and well-connected as Catholics, and had been very active in the Catholic Church as lay workers. They had done a great deal during the charismatic renewal years of the Catholic Church, but they had left and moved on over twenty years before. What we discovered that night was a powerful demon called the 'Catholic spirit,' another principality, a demonic power that specialised in manipulating and controlling this branch of the Kingdom of God. This 'Catholic spirit' had never accepted that this couple had left the Catholic Church, and pursued them relentlessly, hounding them as if they were renegade Catholics who must return. That night when we prayed for them and released them, it was a watershed in their lives. It was as if up to that point they were still spiritually bound to be Catholics, but from that night they were free.

You might ask, "Why did it have power to pursue them? Why could they not just walk away? Others do so." The answer in their case is that they were connected to, and loved by, many priests and nuns, and bishops too, some of whom were relatives, and many were praying religious prayers to have them return. Amongst all of this, some would have continued to pray controlling or emotional prayers, thus empowering a high level of demonic spirit activity.

What I write is not about judging other Christians or denominations. All I am illustrating is that every denomination struggles with this same problem of the leaven that gets mixed into the dough. And we each have to make sure that we keep that leaven out of our own hearts, and do not allow the enemy an opportunity to put some kind of stranglehold on our work as we go along and the work matures.

At the same time, and this is the message of this chapter, we must understand that in *every* city and in *all* denominations, independent churches, and Christian institutions, there are principalities and powers attached to and assigned against these and other kingdom branches, and that these powers seek to manipulate and control. They actively speak into these Christian entities, and are quite capable of speaking, at times, through its people.[2] This demonic spirit activity is in addition to those other principalities and powers that we normally think of as being in or against a city.

And we ought not be surprised about this. Here is Young's Literal Translation of Ephesians 6:12, "...*because we have not the wrestling with blood and flesh, but with the principalities, with the authorities, with the world-rulers of the darkness of this age, with the spiritual things of the evil in the heavenly places...*"

The *"principalities"* and *"authorities"* we are referring to are each individual, personal, intelligent, created spirits; they

---

2 Mark 8:33, Acts 5:3

are fallen angels, fallen authorities, defined by Paul as *"world-rulers of the darkness of this age"* (YLT). Yet we find that, rather than addressing them by a personal name, they will often go by, or at least are very successfully named and dealt with, by the very name of the institution they have infiltrated, or the stronghold they have established. So you have a Presbyterian spirit or a Catholic spirit, and in the case of the Salvation Army there is a strong religious spirit that is commonly referred to as 'the Army spirit' (although this term is assumed by its official users to be referring to the grand way the organization is meant to flourish in the hearts of its people, but in practice it is very often just enthusiastic, but dead, religious tradition.) I know of a number of leaders who have personally come face-to-face with this powerful denominational demon, and had to stand against it in the faith, and discovered it is a genuine demonic power seeking to enforce tradition and conformity.

As a humorous aside, my first church as a Salvation Army officer was in Narrabri, New South Wales. When we arrived, there was not a lot there, and not much had been going on. But we were new and energetic, and the two years we were there saw everything grow by large percentages – worship attendance, Sunday School, women's ministry, special events, new converts, and good increases in financial flow. At the end of two years, we had an official 'inspection' by the Divisional Commander, part of the standard procedure. This meant a full examination and analysis of all the records. The D.C. visited, completed all the records, and asked many questions. We were all on good terms, he was a good and caring man, and he went away to complete his report. I received my copy many weeks later, after we had moved on to our next assignment. His final summary of the work was this sentence: "There is a seemingly good spiritual life in the corps, but it lacks Army spirit." At the time I thought this was an insult, and a contradiction in terms. (How, I thought then, could you have a good spiritual life and lack the right spirit?) Now, I thank God, it is an honour. It was not a contradiction in terms – the Holy Spirit had freedom, the denominational spirit was bound. And by the way, I had led 24 men, many of them alcoholics, some of them prisoners in the local jail, to Christ in those two years.

Denominational spirits are demons. We are not talking about the Holy Spirit, nor the Godly believers in these churches. These institutions are invariably full of wonderful, Christian people, believers who know the Lord – but of course there will also be tares among the wheat.

The Bible speaks sufficiently about the need to be aware of Satan's schemes.[3] So if we honestly think about how a devil would go about scheming against the church, of course he would try to infiltrate so as to manipulate it. To think otherwise is to be naïve. But the church that is alive in the Holy Spirit will fight to gain and maintain ascendency over the powers of darkness, and has been called to do so. This is the natural reading of Ephesians 6:11-18.

Earlier in that same epistle, Paul highlights the fact that rather than fallen powers holding the church in bondage, it is meant to be a case of the church giving orders to the powers. He is obviously speaking of the church filled with grace and love, empowered by the Holy Spirit, yielded to Christ and worshipping God by the Spirit of Christ, and moving as one in faith. This church is appointed to assert truth and exercise authority over these dark rulers and fallen authorities, and in doing so furthers the eternal purpose of God in Christ Jesus: "*His intent was that now, **through the church**, the manifold wisdom of God should be made known to the rulers and authorities in the heavenly realms, according to his eternal purpose that he accomplished in Christ Jesus our Lord*" (Ephesians 3:10-11).

The Masonic Lodge

One of the most entrenched powers in the history of the nation, a religious, occultic power, is the Masonic Lodge. It claims to be a brotherhood, but is a secret society with secret

3 2 Corinthians 2:11, Ephesians 6:11

rituals, secret oaths, secret curses, and secret practices.

The spirit of the Masonic Lodge is extremely religious and therefore can get on famously with branches of the church that are also religious (as against being holy and spiritual). It is of a completely opposite spirit to the Spirit of Jesus Christ, so wherever people try to advance in the things of Christ, that demonic spirit will be opposing them.

It is a well-known fact amongst Spirit-filled pastors and Christian workers that, for some reason that has always been difficult to understand, Masonic power is strong, and often hard to shift. We meet Christians everywhere who, whilst they have never personally been part of the Lodge, had a father or grandfather who had been, and the result has been ongoing spiritual struggles, health issues, and curses in the family. You will find generational sicknesses and all kinds of hindrances including spiritual dullness.

When people pray and renounce the Lodge and the sins of their ancestors, and seek the Lord to be delivered, they go free and healings take place. Yet that can be one of the most difficult things to deal with in the lives of those who are under its oppression, and sometimes people have to deal with it repeatedly to get free. Sometimes you pray and pray yet seem to get nowhere. WHY is that so?

Why does it seem to be so much harder to break Masonic curses off believers who have been under that spirit generationally, than it is to pray and remove other curses which, usually once named and dealt with, are easily ended?

Well consider this: Many denominations have been hand-in-glove with the Masonic Lodge for a very long time. This is tantamount to the Lodge having church approval and blessing. Therefore, ordinary Christian workers find it hard to overcome the spirits and curses of the Lodge, because it has been entrenched, and is protected, by 'official Christian' approval.

You often cannot really shift the Masonic curses without dealing with the denominational spirits first.

The Masonic Lodge was instrumental in the spread of many of the denominations in Australia. With respect to Rockhampton, the Lodge was involved in some denominations moving in and starting here. The same is true of Adelaide, and will be true of many places. There have often been both active and passive agreements between many churches/denominations and the Masonic Lodge. I know of places in Australia where Lodges founded churches and churches founded Lodges. I know of congregations of various denominations that were largely populated by Lodge members. I know of more than one denomination in Rockhampton where most or all of the senior lay leaders and elders were Masons, and this continued for many decades, even to the present time.

My own father and maternal grandfather were Masons, both were Salvation Army bandmasters, both knew the Lord, but didn't have a clue what they had put themselves under. Both suffered the spiritual reverses that it brings, and their children then need to renounce it and break it off to get free. Praise God we can do so, for we have the cross, the shed blood, and the Name of Christ.

What I have described, the historic mixing of Christian churches and their leaders with this highly occultic secret society, and the bringing of the Lodge into the 'bosom' of the church by many, is called syncretism. This is the mixing of two things that ought never be mixed. It is akin to Old Testament Israel worshipping Baal and Ashtoreth, and demons getting into Israel as a result. It is an abomination; it is surrendering to a demonic spirit; it is a doctrine of demons. Whenever a man enters the Lodge and takes the first vow, a veil comes over the eyes of his heart, and he cannot see the Lodge for what it is. But it is powerful occultism dressed up in a religious guise, using much Bible terminology which helps disguise its true nature and makes it appear benign.

Which brings us to the point; the reason the Masonic curse is hard to break off the lives of many believers is because the principalities and powers that enforce Masonic bondage are in league with the principalities and powers that have infiltrated Christian denominations. And besides, the Masonic spirit was what helped many of the denominational spirits get into such places of power in Christian churches in the first place. Can you see it? These are in one accord, they protect each other. What this means is that, in practice, if these 'Christian' denominational spirits are not first bound, they will be standing in agreement with, and 'covering,' the Masonic spirit, and you will find it very difficult to successfully break the power of the Masonic curse.

But if in prayer and declaration we first bind and renounce such denominational spirits, then the Masonic spirit is isolated, and is then only just one more religious spirit. It will have lost its covering protection, and therefore much of its power.

Such declarations (if made effective with authority and faith) are an essential part of finding power in our prayers to save our cities. When we rebuke and bind these principalities, it is not people or church organisations we are addressing – we are dealing directly with demonic principalities, so that God's people can go free.

This difficult subject can be easily misunderstood and found offensive by some, but my reason for discussing these things is to bring light to darkness, and make clear this reality in the spirit realm. Ephesians 5:11 says, *"Have nothing to do with the fruitless deeds of darkness, but rather expose them."*

Satan seeks to infiltrate everywhere, and in some cases has developed great controls in denominations. It is not, however, a one-sided confrontation; the church has many victories too, but it is as Paul said, *"we wrestle... with principalities."*

The Prayer We Prayed in Rockhampton

As previously recounted in Chapter 1, following the teaching of this material on institutional spirits one Sunday, which I called, *The State of the War*, my son David and I prayed that evening around Rockhampton for the churches. This broke the long drought, but only over the city. It began to rain within an hour of finishing, and we had good rain four times a week for four months. Rockhampton became the "island of green" I told of earlier.

What was that prayer? It was a brief prayer, and took less than a minute. I took authority over the principality, the high-level demonic spirit that had infiltrated the denomination of which each local church was a part, and bound the spirit, to cut it off from affecting the local congregation and the city. It was as basic as that. And we drove on to the next. I prayed this prayer for all the churches, and as I did, it became increasingly clear these spirits were not all the same; they had personality and strong traits peculiar to what they had established in specific denominations.

It amazed me that it brought the rain, where much prayer had not. But it made one of the great issues we have to come to grips with very clear: the nation around us, its economy and well-being, are directly affected by the spiritual state of the Church. When the Church is bound, especially bound up with denominational division and dead tradition, the nation suffers, and with it our cities and towns, our farmers, our economy, and our families.

When others in a number of places duplicated what I did (i.e. they went around their towns and prayed to bind the denominational spirits), they got the same outcome – much needed rain!

But the pastor I mentioned from N.S.W., who shared his story at my school, knew nothing of this. He had been led by the Lord to walk around his town and pray relative to the churches too – but was given a prayer that had an entirely different point. It was "to cut off the denominational *claims* over the town."

And the astounding outcome for him was the same. The rains began, and the town became green – but only his town. The state remained in drought.

Drought

The issue of the heavens being open or closed, and of whether or not the natural and spiritual blessings we are supposed to receive are freely flowing, has a great deal to do with denominational life. The divided nature of an institutionalised Body of Christ, with its sectarian spirit, exclusivity, superior attitudes, and the like, along with its strong territorial claims expressed in attitudes and prayers, all embedded in the traditional institutional structures of the church, see to it that the heavens are often locked up, and the Church in many ways is bound by dark powers – all because of the 'agreement' and 'consent' of our flesh.

And it is this religiosity and tradition of much of what passes for Christianity, combined with jealousy and selfish ambition in Christian leaders, all in a format of independence from one another, that plays into Satan's schemes and locks up the heavens.

We must all take warning, and be repentant, for James said, "… *where you have envy and selfish ambition, there you find disorder and every evil practice*" (James 3:16).

Rain

I went to Cambodia in the dry season some 10 years ago. Cambodia's dry season lasts seven months and the rainy season five months. In the rainy season there is water everywhere, but in the dry season it's a dust bowl. The land is generally flat with rice paddies in every direction. I arrived in the middle of the dry, and took a taxi to the Pastors' conference where I was to be the guest speaker.

I had been there teaching this same large group the year

before, and covered many matters of general importance, but this time I knew my assignment was to use the whole conference to teach the principles of the current apostolic reformation of the Church. In particular, the heart of my message was to be about city eldership and the essential unity of the Body of Christ.

Attending were about a hundred and fifty pastors from all over Cambodia, although the majority were from Phnom Penh, the capital. Remember, this was in the middle of the dry season, when it never rains. Sitting in the taxi on the way to the conference, the Lord said to me, "I'm going to make it rain all over the land of Cambodia, as a sign, that if they believe what you tell them about city eldership, I will pour out my spirit over the whole land of Cambodia."

When you are told things like that you need to have a little courage. So I stood up in the first meeting and declared, "The Lord has said that He's going to make it rain over the whole land of Cambodia as a sign, that if you believe what I am about to tell you about city eldership, He will pour out His Spirit all over the land."

It rained that night, it rained the next night, and on the third day it rained all over Cambodia. And on the fourth day, with the conference over, we drove through several provinces on ministry visits, and saw water lying everywhere like you wouldn't believe.

CHAPTER SIX

The
Disparate State

Claims and Counter-Claims in the Body of Christ

'The entire law is summed up in a single command:
"Love your neighbor as yourself."
If you keep on biting and devouring each other,
watch out or you will be destroyed by each other.'
(Galatians 5:14-15)

I raise here a difficult matter that must be addressed for the liberty of the people of God and the freedom of our cities. And we will need to have a good heart in considering these things. The matter of serious concern is the spiritual damage caused by otherwise well-meaning people making territorial claims, often with exclusive attitudes and an independent spirit – and the inappropriateness of doing so.

The Gold Coast

Let me give you a little background. Some years ago I was to conduct a conference on the Gold Coast. We had been praying about it for several months, and not long before the event the Lord began to give us quite graphic visions and words.

What we were shown, for example, were visions of many lines tightly crisscrossing the Gold Coast. What was being portrayed was gridlock, not unlike a traffic snarl. The city was locked up somehow, locked up so rigidly that nothing could move spiritually. And what was it that caused all this spiritual gridlock? It was the long years of multiple claims and counterclaims of pastors, churches, Christians, intercessors, and prophets – all claiming the Gold Coast for the success of their own ministries – i.e. for themselves.

This was a city to which a great many ministries had gone to plant churches over the years, and many people had laid claims in prayer, as in; "I claim this city for Jesus, I claim the families of this city for Jesus. I claim converts from this city for Jesus." But the literal meaning of the words they speak is not what goes out into the spirit realm. What goes out is whatever is in the spirit of that person. It may be selfish ambition, especially if they love themselves but don't love the rest of the Body. If they have no respect for other churches, but assert they are there to start a 'real' church, evil has just been laid on the city. And it's these evil claims that serve to spiritually gridlock cities all over the world because individual Christian leaders are laying claims on them – quite apart from the problem of denominational claims.

Anyone who has a background in prayer, church planting, and pioneering, would know that it has been common thinking in Christian circles, especially when starting new work, to claim the ground in the name of Jesus. Probably like the majority of other Christians who pray warfare or faith-type prayers, most of us have used this kind of expression, i.e. claiming something, in our prayers.

But on the whole this causes problems rather than solving them. There are better and more biblical alternatives to this type of prayer, which I will come to. In our prayer meetings concerning the Gold Coast, the one clear word I heard from the Lord in relation to the Church there was, "Disparate."

The 'Disparate' Condition

In giving this uniquely descriptive word, the Holy Spirit was describing the spiritual state of the Body of Christ in that city. It was in a disparate condition; they were a disparate people.

But I hasten to add: this is *typical* of the state of the church and cities all over the world.

I thought I knew what 'disparate' meant; something like separate and divided, not joined together but instead scattered. But I've always found that when the Lord gives me one specific word, the dictionary definition will give me clear light on what the Lord is communicating. So I went home and looked up the dictionary, and discovered a very important piece of information – that the word 'disparate' means that not only are the pieces separate and scattered, but more: it is not possible to join any pieces that are in a disparate condition because they are of a *different kind*, such that they *cannot* be joined. It is not possible for them to be joined because they have a different nature! It is like having a half-inch nut and a half-inch bolt but the thread is different so you can't join them. The Lord said that was the spiritual state of affairs in that city.

You could ask yourself, as I did, "How could that possibly be true concerning the Body of Christ, because aren't we all one in Christ?" We believe the same doctrine, we preach the same Bible, we pray similar prayers, we believe the same promises, and we have the same Saviour. There are large numbers of people in every city who are born of the Spirit, exercise spiritual gifts, preach the same gospel and believe exactly the same things. How then could they possibly be described as being in a *disparate* state?

The truth is, they do not really believe the same things! Yes, they may well believe the same things about God, the Bible, and the gospel, **but they do not believe the same things about themselves, and about each other.**

We are all full of beliefs, and if we asked any Christian to write down a list of their Christian beliefs, they might write down a dozen things, such as: Christ is the Son of God; the Bible was written by the inspiration of the Holy Spirit; and so on. But in addition to what we would each record, we all have in our hearts thousands of other beliefs, both conscious and subconscious. These include beliefs about ourselves, about the church down the road, about the pastor of that church, and so on. And many people who begin to plant a church have, as their starting point, a belief that no-one else in the city has done a great job, but they think they will be the ones to get the job done.

Their starting point is almost never an acknowledgement that God already has wonderful people in the city, nor have they a quest to find out who was appointed to preach the gospel and build the church before they arrived in order to build a meaningful relationship with them. Rather, their starting point is too often those underlying assumptions that care not about other people, only that they are there to build *their* church.

These are beliefs of the *heart*. There will be many of these, such as the belief that they are better than other people and have better doctrine, better worship, better promises, better prophecies, and better faith. And if they are not carrying an assumption that says 'we are better than others,' they will often have the alternative assumption, which is that other people are not as good as us!

There is no denying that human beings – and I am talking about born-again, Spirit-filled believers – are too often full of such beliefs. These are *fleshly* beliefs.

Fleshly Belief Systems

Too much of the work of the church is being done out of such fleshly beliefs instead of a proper discernment of the Body of Christ and of the will of God.

Consequently, when church workers have, for example, gone out to prayer-walk the streets, claiming a city for Christ, it creates the following problem. What goes out into the spirit realm is not the literal meaning of their words. If it was just the literal meaning of their words that would be well and good, because they are saying, "I claim this city for Christ." **But what actually goes out into the spirit realm is whatever happens to be in that person's spirit.** So if they're full of beliefs about being better than other people, the claim they make has the spirit of that belief system behind it; which means they are claiming that this city will come to Christ but will join them and follow them and will not follow those who were there before they arrived. Of course this is not usually what people are consciously thinking, but I can tell you it is rooted deeply in the heart desires of a great many.

It is even worse when a person who feels called to a town to start a new church has a heart that doesn't care about those who were there before them, doesn't take any interest in whether other ministers do have the Word of God, or whether the Spirit of the Lord is with them or not, and doesn't care that others have poured their lives into the city. They just want to be a success, to get a following, and to make a mark. Such a person may or may not be motivated by a true call from the Lord and a sense of having been appointed and sent by Him. For there are those driven by selfish ambition and envy, which things hide in the human heart and are hard to measure. Usually those with such motives don't know they're there. But when such a person goes out and walks the street (or simply prays at home) and claims the city for Christ, what they lay upon the city is not a claim for Christ at all. Rather, laid upon that city is their selfish ambition to control the city. Out of this envy is established a curse that goes out seeking to cut down and hinder the work of other Christians in the city.

Consider the effect created when a pastor, driven by a competitive spirit, comes to town with great ambitions to build a church and constantly claims not only the town, and his leadership of it, but the souls, the wealth, the success, the growth, and the progress. And he claims the families; this is a common prayer. We are not dealing here with just the lunatic fringe; this is a common way that people pray. This behavior gridlocks the city spiritually so that nobody gets anywhere.

And perhaps worse again is where good people – committed, hard-working, well-meaning, faith-filled people – are there for the Lord, but not getting on with each other, i.e. not agreeing with each other, and not serving each other.

What is the basic call of God upon all believers, and especially on the leaders of the people of God? It is to serve one another! Remember Jesus told his disciples, *"The kings of the Gentiles lord it over them; and those who exercise authority over them call themselves Benefactors. But you are not to be like that. Instead, the greatest among you should be like the youngest, and the one who rules like the one who serves"* (Luke 22:25-26).

When church leaders come to a city but remain total strangers to one another whilst at the same time laying claims over a city, they are 'lording it over' their brethren. Rather, it should be that if anyone feels they are to be a leader, they must come with an attitude of, 'I'm here to serve my brothers and sisters.' How that is best applied is in serving the other pastors/leaders in the city (they are the "brothers and sisters"), and being there to help make other people successful. **This is a completely opposite point of view from the all too common belief system out of which many operate when they go to plant or lead a church.**

And that is why we have many of the problems we do in the Body of Christ. Do you think this is an extreme statement? Then consider for a moment Paul's concern expressed in 1 Corinthians 11:29-31, *"For anyone who eats and drinks without recognizing the body of the Lord eats and drinks judgment on himself. That is why many among you are weak and sick, and a number of you have fallen asleep. But if we judged ourselves, we would not come under judgment."*

The Problem We Have

Now if Christian leaders have basically righteous values and a good heart, but do make lots of claims even though well-meaning, you might have nothing worse than just some degree of spiritual gridlock – with its attendant struggle for freedom imposed upon everybody.

But if a Christian leader happens to be quite competitive and striving, and out of that lays strong claims on a city, then what you end up with is a curse on the city, and very active witchcraft. These kinds of leaders are often insecure, but almost always operating out of covetousness and selfish ambition. And if they are envious of what others have, or jealous of the success of others (an attitude of *resentment* toward others is a symptom of jealousy), this empowers a hate-filled murderous spirit. And if they are also driven with a large degree of personal self-discipline, then they will be working at their 'faith-claims' every day, which means a big struggle for others, especially for the objects of their resentments.

This becomes a typical case, where someone in Christian leadership is actually empowering witchcraft, flattening the rest of the Body of Christ, and doing it all in the name of Jesus. They do this by claiming the city, claiming the power, claiming leadership, claiming the families and the wealth, whilst all the while in their spirit they desire, in arrogance or ignorance, to draw all this to themselves. If that claim stands (i.e. the resulting spirit activity in the city is not recognized for what it is and refuted by leaders with authority), then it has the power to rip out of the hands of the families of the city and the people of God much of the inheritance that was rightfully theirs. The result: everyone has less, and everyone struggles more.

Where you have God's people at work in the fellowship of various churches, ideally they are seeking to build up Christian family life and the work of the gospel in the city, seeking to build the strength and commonwealth of the Kingdom of God. But when someone who has no great respect for other ministries, but in their own mind thinks they are 'God's answer' for the town, proceeds to lay strong, fleshly 'faith-claims' over all the families, converts, wealth, growth, and increase as their own, we have a seriously debilitating effect upon the churches.

Here's why: Such a claim goes out into the spirit realm and establishes a 'legal' position, that if all these things belong to the 'claimant' as the rightful owner, then they do not belong to any other person or church. As a consequence, dark forces, i.e. principalities and powers, can and do use this as their spiritual authority to deny growth and success to all others.

Basically, such a claimant is a thief, as is Satan who manipulates such claims. Spiritual claims such as these empower unclean spirits to go against churches and take away from Christian ministries and Godly families what was meant to be rightfully theirs by the will of God. We need to understand how dangerous this is, and correct our attitudes and methods.

These kinds of claims do affect everyone. They affect you, they affect the Church as a whole in the city, and they affect the life of the city itself. These things work to bring the city into bondage and the church into oppression. I will here discuss what the solution is to the problem of people who make these kinds of claims, and then go on to list the healthy, life-giving, biblical Christian practices we ought to follow rather than operating out of claims.

Difficult Lessons

I learned these lessons through difficult experiences in our city. There was a time in our church when, despite being surrounded by many wonderful opportunities, and with a sense that all of them could and should be taken up, there was at the same time a strong feeling of threat and oppression.

I prayed into this for many weeks, and came to see that the bigger part of this heavy spiritual resistance and hateful opposition was the result of claims that had been laid upon the city. During a two-day drive to conduct a ministry weekend in

Wamberal, N.S.W., I was trying to listen to the Lord on these things. I was going over earnest questions before the Lord, because I had become conscious of the very self-centred and ambitious claims being made by one of the pastors and his team over our city.

I carried a burden, too, for another minister and church who were close friends. This particular church, which had been healthy and had brought many to Christ, had been doing well for many years but was now struggling. People started leaving, things went downhill, and they ended up having to close some of their services. Eventually the pastor, a good man with a genuine call, became really sick, and finally left the ministry. All this was the direct result of the ambitious, driven (I could say vicious) 'prayer claims' of a pastor, who led the very competitive culture of the church he had established to strongly claim that area as theirs. This kind of spirituality is witchcraft and it empowers demons.

Unfortunately, the pastor who was my friend, and with whom I (and others) met every week, did not believe in this kind of spiritual warfare. I raised it several times, explained what was causing his catastrophes and the kind of prayer needed, and explained how we had prevented it from affecting us. I offered to come to his office with other pastors and help him deal with it in prayer, but he couldn't see it. He did not believe the diagnosis of what was causing the problems, and he did not believe in the kind of prayer that was needed to solve them. Consequently, there was no opportunity to apply the antidote for his church's decline and his own ongoing illness.

In contrast to this, we had a family in our church that were committed to apostolic ministry, and had felt led to step out in faith and serve full-time without salary, trusting the Lord to provide for them. This family had done well financially for the first several years of this arrangement, but then came a two-year period where financial things became a struggle and they couldn't seem to get ahead. One Saturday night this couple were up late praying about it, and in seeking the Lord they realised their house was in the neighbourhood, virtually in the shadow of, the church that was making strong territorial claims, declaring that part of the city to be theirs. So they prayed and cut off the claims, including the financial claims, that were being made over the area they lived in, and immediately their finances shifted gear. They've been doing well ever since, continuing to prosper.

These kinds of claims, if driven by someone ambitious who has discipline behind that ambition, become more and more demonic as time goes on. It becomes an increasingly stronger curse on the whole Body of Christ.

Earnest Questions of the Lord

It was because of all this that I was so earnestly asking the Lord what we should do. I spent two hours at the wheel, whilst driving in Queensland from Miles to Goondiwindi, staring into space as it were, seeking to understand the nature of claims and what to do about it.

In years past it had seemed normal to pray in faith and claim a city for Christ, although I had always taught that when people make claims in Christ's name, what goes out is whatever is in their spirit. But I had always maintained that if in their heart was a sincere desire for the advance of the Kingdom, and if they were genuinely desirous that Christ's will be done and all of God's people blessed, then it was of grace when they claimed a city for Christ. But now, I was not so sure.

There are many good people who do have a pure heart of love, who really do want God's will to be done and want to see God's people blessed, and so their prayers are not in that sense harmful. We can be sure there will be many praying who are not praying out of a fleshly motive – although at the same time it is difficult, if not impossible, for us to really know our own motives, which are often *mixed* motives.

I pondered, then, whether or not *all* claims were evil?

Yet there are people who do have *true claims*, who have been appointed to positions of leadership and authority and who would have a 'right' to a claim. And there are also people who have been cheated out of their (spiritual) inheritance who could have rightful claims, claims that are just. And God is a God of justice. So I conclude that there are some claims that are righteous in themselves, and there are some people who are righteous in making claims.

But here is the problem. **When dealing with spiritual warfare, you have to operate out of an opposite spirit or you cannot win the battle.** If someone with an unrighteous attitude claims the City of Rockhampton, and then another person with a righteous spirit also claims the city, this is not going to win any battles. In other words, **you can't fight claims with counter-claims**. You will not get anywhere taking a position that says someone else's claim was evil but your claim is good.

Even if you are the one person in a hundred who is totally pure of heart, and wanting just what God wants for the city, you cannot fight the battle that way. I cannot stress enough that the only way to win this kind of battle is to have an opposite spirit.

I was thinking all this through on that long drive to Wamberal, pondering the things that were coming against us, and the fact that many of our people at that time were experiencing sleep deprivation, headaches, and sickness. We were seeing all kinds of symptoms that were hard to throw off. Even when we cut off the claims, things were not shifting enough and we weren't getting very far. Basically my question was, "Lord, how do I really get free from the claims of these people, and how do we properly deal with them?"

Somewhere between Goodiwindi, Qld, and Moree N.S.W., I heard the answer of the Lord: **"Relinquish your own claims on Rockhampton."**

Relinquishing Claims

At first I wondered if this meant that all claims were evil after all, but I realised it wasn't as simple as that. The Lord didn't say, "Repent of the claims, or renounce them." He said, "Relinquish them." We are not meant to hold other people in debt to us, so to relinquish is fine because we can take a position of giving freedom to all other people. I like the Scripture that says of God in Psalm 47:4, *"He chose our inheritance for us."* We don't have to go out and demand our inheritance, claiming 'This suburb is mine!' 'This city is mine!' or 'This farm or shop is mine!'

Instead we can take the beautiful position of thanking the Lord, with great assurance of faith, that He has chosen our inheritance for us. And we then ask Him to give us our inheritance.

There's more power in this, and there's more peace in it, too. We sleep better at night. But in taking a 'claim' position in prayer, believing that the only way to get your prayers answered and to build something for God is to claim and claim and keep claiming until you have it, results in a prayer that is based on your own works. In other words, it involves your own ability to keep speaking the words and keep holding on and keep fighting until things happen. Let me tell you, that isn't real prayer; not if you're holding a subconscious belief that you have to perform to get the results. And please don't think you've got to perform to get results with God. No, with the Lord we rest, and believe. The purpose of prayer is to bring us to that place of faith where we find complete rest, where we know that God has heard our prayer.

When I heard the Lord say, "Relinquish your own claims," I proceeded to do so right then and there. The moment I did, I felt the whole battle shift. Then I was able to cut off the claims of other people and find freedom.

We are not, by this, cursing other people. We simply have to recognise that, whether we know people are praying this way or not, we need to release our homes, families, finances, and church life from the claims that have been laid upon the city in which we live. We need to pray for the release of our churches and our people, and quit making claims; quit relying on our own strong, rugged individualism to get results, and turn our hearts back to do the things that the Lord tells us to do.

An Opposite Spirit

The biggest *curse* on our cities is not abortion, or brothels, or pornography, or gambling, or addictions, even though those things are evil. Rather, it's the illegitimate and illicit claims of Christian leaders who puff themselves up, put themselves in Christ's seat, and say, 'This is mine!' – because it locks up the people of God from doing what they need to do with the gospel and it leaves the city wide-open for all this other evil to come in.

There are keys in James 3:15-18 that enable us to sort this out, and to enjoy much greater freedom in our homes, churches, and cities. Verse 15 says, "*Such wisdom does not come down from heaven.*" What is this *'wisdom'* being referred to? In the previous verse James was speaking of fleshly ambition and envy, and he's about to name them again in verse 16, "*Such 'wisdom' does not come down from heaven, but is earthly, unspiritual, of the devil. For where you have envy and selfish ambition, there you find disorder and every evil practice.*"

I have long known that wherever there is selfish ambition or envy at work in the hearts of Christians, the door is open for every demonic power imaginable to come into the church and wreak havoc. And here you have it in black and white, in Holy Writ, as inspired by the Holy Spirit.

James continues (v17-18), "*But the wisdom that comes from heaven is first of all pure, then peace loving, considerate, submissive, full of mercy and good fruit, impartial and sincere. Peace makers who sow in peace raise a harvest of righteousness."*

To sow in peace means, at the least, not operating out of selfish ambition and envy, which means no more fleshly claims. An opposite spirit is always required, and the result is that the power of the devil falls away.

In the centre of verse 17 are two great key words; *'considerate'* and *'submissive.'* This is the wisdom of heaven in our dealings with other Christians. And to build the case further for the need to have a different attitude to the works of other Christians in our cities, consider also the defining word then added by James, *'impartial.'* This is to be the value system of our hearts, held by all ministers of Christ toward each other, and toward all the churches of Christ in the city – *'impartial!'*

And the apostle Paul's declaration of the same truth is this: *"so that there should be no division in the body, but that its parts should have equal concern for each other"* (1 Corinthians 12:25). **Equal Concern for each other!**

Spiritually Joined

But we find, in church life in most cities in Australia, the churches have very little to do with each other. Yet even though not mixing with each other very often, we actually have *invisible* dealings with each other every single day – because spiritually we are *joined*. The attitude of your church affects the others, and their attitude affects you. If you don't want someone's carnal attitude having a nasty affect on you, then you must have a healthy, holy, biblical, gracious attitude towards them. You have to be of an opposite spirit. And if you want to walk in the wisdom of heaven, you need to be considerate towards other people.

Suppose you have the assignment of planting a new church in a city where there are already, amongst others, evangelical and Pentecostal churches. Amongst them are Godly people that the Lord has planted, and to whom He has given promises, and whom He wants to bless. **What would a considerate, impartial, having 'equal concern' person do?**

Do you think that, out of consideration, the first thing might be to go and offer your friendship, your service, your support, and your love, to others? Would it not be, at the least, beholden upon you to recognise that God had appointed other ministers to the city before He had appointed you? Should you not recognize that there is one Body, just as there is one Lord and one faith? That there is, according to Jesus' Revelation to John, only one golden lampstand in the city?

Would you not at least make yourself known to key leaders and offer an explanation of your position – "I believe the Lord has sent me here to do a work. But I want to know you and serve in love, not wanting in any way to harm your work or that of others. Can I walk with you and learn from you?" Wouldn't taking such a completely different attitude result in more blessing over all the church? Should a new church grow by purposefully ripping the innards out of twenty other churches to do so, as some indeed have done, or is it more important that the whole city and the whole Body of Christ is blessed, and that real believers in the city might grow from a thousand to ten thousand?

With two of my associate leaders, David Hood and Tony Ponicke, I used to meet regularly with a group of pastors in our city (we still do, but the group has changed and advanced). One day we met with six or seven others at St. Andrews Presbyterian Church, and as part of the conversation I said, "If we, the leaders of our churches, would walk together as a people, if we would love each other and knit our hearts, then every one would have a church of a thousand instead of a hundred." But the problem is, people don't overcome their self-protected positions so as to make themselves vulnerable enough to do what is good and best for the Body of Christ.

We change this, but not by thinking everyone else needs to change whilst we ourselves stay pretty much the same. We have to take the lowly position, the position of being servants of all. We will be the ones to be considerate, to be peace-loving and submissive to our brethren. We will offer to help and serve and express our love in our dealings with them every day. Why do I say 'in our dealings with them every day?' I mean in our prayers and in what we believe about them. We will be considerate because this is *"the wisdom that comes from"* above and is *"heavenly."* With this sort of approach we have some hope of being those *"peacemakers who sow in peace,"* and who according to the words of James 3:18, reap that *"harvest of righteousness."*

A Better Way of Praying

If, then, we should not make claims, we need to get back to some honest prayer and listening, and be freedom-giving towards all in these prayers. Here's the instruction of 1 Timothy 2:1-4, *"I urge then, first of all, that requests, prayers, intercession and thanksgiving be made for everyone, for kings and all those in authority, that we may live* (here's the result...) *peaceful and quiet lives in all godliness and holiness. This is good, and pleases God our Saviour who wants all men to be saved and to come to a knowledge of the truth."*

The making of claims may not have been the bigger part of your praying. But since you do pray and live and work in your city, what are the more biblical alternatives. In fact there are a great many other ways to take up effective prayer. You have a huge opportunity to do good.

1. Ask God to Give You Your Inheritance in the City.

We referred earlier to Psalm 47:4, which says it is God who chooses our inheritance for us. Psalm 16:6 also helps us to exult in this faith, *"The boundary lines have fallen for me in pleasant places; surely I have a delightful inheritance."* God knows how to give a rich inheritance, even a double-portion to people whose hearts He can trust, and whose hearts are greatly enlarged by love. So you can certainly ask for your inheritance. My experience in life has been that every time you pray like this, something starts to shift. Remember James 4:2, *"You do not have, because you do not ask God."*

2. Strongly Believe Promises.

If God has given you a promise for the city, you can believe that promise. For example, Jeremiah 33:9, *"Then this city will bring me renown, joy, praise and honor before all nations on earth that hear of all the good things I do for it; and they will be in awe and will tremble at the abundant prosperity and peace I provide for it."* What would be wrong with believing that promise, and walking about the streets saying, "Lord, that's your promise for the city. We believe, that is what you are going to do." That is better than a claim any day. It is the better way of faith rather than of dead works.

3. Make a Declaration.

This point is probably as close to a claim as you may get, but it's not a claim. Isn't it better to declare that, "This city is Jesus Christ's," rather than to say, "I claim this city for the Lord Jesus." A truthful declaration with faith is a power for good.

4. Commit to Petition and Supplication

Then there is always the daily opportunity to get into genuinely serious prayer, in a spirit of supplication. This is the making of many requests of God, which the Bible tells us to do, but with faith, believing He hears and answers your prayers. Supplication is that earnest, pleading prayer that will not be denied.

Consider the example of Hannah: *'In bitterness of soul Hannah wept much and prayed to the Lord... Hannah replied, "I am a woman who is deeply troubled... I was pouring out my soul to the Lord... I have been praying here out of my great anguish and grief." Eli answered, "Go in peace, and may the God of Israel grant you what you have asked of him"* ' (1 Samuel 1:10, 15-17).

Furthermore, we have the example of the Lord Jesus: *"During the days of Jesus' life on earth, he offered up prayers and petitions with loud cries and tears to the one who could save him from death, and he was heard because of his reverent submission"* (Hebrews 5:7).

5. Have a Heart for Intercession

Intercession is where we specifically plead for others – in this case, for other churches and the freedom of the people of God, as well as for the whole city, asking God to do great things. As Paul instructs: *"pray in the Spirit on all occasions with all kinds of prayers and requests. With this in mind, be alert and always keep on praying for all the saints"* (Ephesians 6:18).

We should note well Paul's directive here, *"for **all** the saints."*

Indeed, *"impartial"* is the *"wisdom that comes from heaven,"* said James.

6. You Can Prophesy.

Inspired utterance in the form of prophecy, with faith,[1] is powerfully effective. Many are more gifted with this than they realise, and instruction in speaking by the Holy Spirit and faith would soon bring release of this giftedness. In faith and by the Holy Spirit, there could be much prophecy the like of: "The Lord says, 'I will do good to this city and save it. The churches in it I will bring into great freedom. You will see an increasing harvest of souls for the Kingdom, and find joy in your inheritance.'"

7. You Must Command Blessing

I have dealt with this subject extensively in my book, *The Spirit of Sonship*, a textbook on relationships in the ministry of Christ. But simply put, blessing is always commanded. A

---

1 Romans 12:6, 1 Corinthians 14:1, Revelation 11:6.

blessing is not a prayer, nor a prophecy, it is a proclamation! This is seen in Psalm 133:3 *"For there the LORD has commanded the blessing, life forevermore"* (ESV). Or as the New International Version translates, it is a bestowal!

We see this, too, in the writings of the apostles. They were always commanding the blessings of *"grace"* and *"peace"* over the churches. This was their duty, just as it was the duty of the Aaronic priesthood to command blessing over Israel every day, with similar emphases on grace and peace, as recorded in Numbers 6:22-27:

> *'The Lord said to Moses, "Tell Aaron and his sons,*
> *'This is how you are to bless the Israelites. Say to them:*
> *" ' "The Lord bless you and keep you;*
> *the Lord make his face shine upon you and be gracious to you;*
> *the Lord turn his face toward you and give you peace." '*
> *"So they will put my name on the Israelites, and I will bless them." '*

All of us have the power to bless. Solomon wrote that *"the tongue has the power of life and death,"*[2] and Paul commanded us to *"bless and do not curse."*[3] To bless is a spiritual duty in the priestly ministry of all Christian believers.

Competition and the Spirit of Witchcraft

But how opposed to all of this, and how spiritually negative, are the kind of claims that are being reinforced by somebody extremely ambitious who has an attitude that they are better than other people. This always empowers a spirit of witchcraft.

It needs to be dealt with resolutely, as this spirit of witchcraft brings with it the oppressions of witchcraft. These begin as a loss of vision and motivation, you may feel flat and can't be bothered. If you find yourself struggling, going through

---

2 Proverbs 18:21
3 Romans 12:14

days, weeks, or months of feeling tired and lacklustre, low in motivation and lacking discipline, you probably need to deal with a spirit of witchcraft.

When pastors or churches have a 'free enterprise' mindset that believes all competition is good, which some do, and see this as the model for building their own 'great' churches, rather than seeing themselves as there to help other people build Christ's church, this spirit of competition easily becomes an evil thing.

If a pastor is driven by ambition to claim it all for 'himself,' that spirit of competition produces a spirit of death. In this way, a death-dealing spirit of witchcraft is authorised to come against families and churches to rob and destroy. We saw this at work back in the nineties, in a period where numbers of women in our church suffered miscarriages. We didn't understand at the time what it was, but eventually, through prayer, we discovered it to be a spirit of death that had come against us, activated by a spirit of competition rife in a couple of other churches in the city.

This spirit of competition at work always has two effects. Firstly, it aids and abets coven witchcraft. There are always active covens of witches, sorcerers, and the like that meet regularly, deceived into doing satanic bidding. Let me be plain: in addition to whatever else they do, they are out there sending incantations, curses, and demons against pastors, churches, Christian marriages, and Christian families.

When the churches are in unity, coven witchcraft has no effectual power against them. But when a spirit of competition, or criticism, gossip, slander, resentment, or jealousy is at work in pastors or churches, these give authority and access to the power of witchcraft. Suddenly, coven witchcraft starts having an oppressive effect. Fortunately, we have grace to deal with this, but it means war in the spirit realm when other Christians are 'authorising' witchcraft.

The Bible's Extensive Warnings

The Bible warns extensively about the dangers that come from the sins of our mouths. David in the Psalms speaks often of the suffering, both physical and psychological, that results from the words and attitudes of companions and other associates.[4] James calls our speech *"a world of evil among the parts of the body,"* says it is *"set on fire by hell"*, and declares it *"a restless evil"* (James 3:6, 8).

Bear in mind, however, that whatever comes out of the mouth has also come out of the heart, as Jesus made clear: *'(Jesus) went on: "What comes out of a man is what makes him 'unclean.' For from within, out of men's hearts, come evil thoughts... envy, slander, arrogance... All these evils come from inside and make a man 'unclean'" '* (Mark 7:20-23). Knowing this, we must understand not only the danger, and evil, of what we *say*, but of what we *think* and *assume* about other Christians, ministers, and churches. For what we *assume* is what is in the *heart*.

In the light of what we have discussed about claims, selfish ambition, envy, etc., and the destructive power of the tongue, read thoughtfully the following passage from David's anguished prayer, and note the pertinent significance of the bold words and phases to our subject of the city we live in:

> *"9 Confuse the* **wicked**, *O Lord, confound their* **speech**, *for I see* **violence and strife** *in the* **city**.
>
> *10* **Day and night they prowl about** *on its walls;* **malice and abuse are within it**.
> *11* **Destructive forces are at work in the city;** **threats and lies** *never leave its streets*.
> *12 If an enemy were insulting me, I could endure it; if a foe were raising himself against me, I could hide from him.*
> *13* **But it is you, a man like myself,** *my* **companion,** *my close* **friend,**

---

4 For example, Psalms 140:3, Psalms 59:7, Psalm 55:21, and many others.

*14 with whom I once enjoyed sweet **fellowship** as we walked with the throng at **the house of God**."* (Psalms 55:9-14)

The Wisdom of Solomon

Solomon wrote, *"With their mouths the godless destroy their neighbours, but through knowledge the righteous escape. When the righteous prosper, the city rejoices; when the wicked perish, there are shouts of joy. Through the blessing of the upright a city is exalted, but by the mouth of the wicked it is destroyed. Whoever derides their neighbour has no sense, but the one who has understanding holds their tongue"* (Proverbs 11:9-12).

Who are these *"godless"* who with their *"mouths"* destroy others, specifically their *"neighbours?"* And who are these *"neighbours?"* Very often, these *"godless"* are amongst us in the church world, and it is then other Christian workers who happen to be their *"neighbours."* Anyone who makes their way in life or ministry by a 'faith' that assumes that other churches or church workers don't count for much, that disdains them, and has no desire for their well-being above his or her own, but relentlessly pursues in an exclusive way their own success, is certainly included in the scope of this Scripture.

Evil Workers and False Brothers

Christians making fleshly claims in the city out of selfish ambition and envy are pursuing a *"godless"* path. They are, I think, included amongst those Paul referred to as *"evil workers."*[5] Yes, they will have a glowing 'testimony,' and say they love the Lord; they worship, and preach the gospel; but they are doing evil work, and by biblical definition are *"evil workers,"* and may be *"false brothers."*

Paul, in outlining innumerable threats he was constantly exposed to, cited at the culmination of his list, *"in danger from false brothers"* (2 Corinthians 11:26). Our danger from this

---

5 Philippians 3:2 (NASB, HCSB, YLT, KJV, ASV)

source is no less an important issue for us as for Paul, or the church in any age. Other dangers may come and go, but this we need to be aware of at all times, and all the while keeping a pure heart – always forgiving, never living out of cynicism, and never motivated by seeking to find fault in others. We must, nevertheless, be able to recognise the condition for what it is, and guard the church and the city whenever it occurs.

Here's a poignant Bible example of both aspects of what I am saying, i.e. the problem occurring, and the necessary defense of the church: *"some false brothers had infiltrated our ranks to spy on the freedom we have in Christ Jesus and to make us slaves. We did not give in to them for a moment, so that the truth of the gospel might remain with you"* (Galatians 2:4-5).

What about the term, *"evil workers?"* I know it occurs, as such, in just one place in the New Testament (Philippians 3:2), and in that context is referring specifically to Judaizers who want to pervert the gospel by preaching circumcision. I am aware, too, that it is translated more generically, such as *"those men who do evil,"* or *"those evildoers,"* in some of the modern translations; but the original language is more specific than this, and the generic terms only serve to emphasise the point in any case.

Therefore, enough is said across many contexts in the gospels and the epistles for us to recognise a truth, and a valid terminology. Much is said about false brothers, false teachers, false prophets, false apostles, and evil deeds, threats to the truth, spys in our midst, etc., for us to realise we have a big picture, with specific problems. It is clear, then, the term does have a wide application, much wider than the immediate context of Philippians 3.

Surely in this matter we can be mature adults, and very clear about something: the danger of false brothers that Paul said he was constantly exposed to was embodied in some who claimed to be gospel workers, and appeared to be greater preachers than

Paul. In other words, they presented themselves as ministers of Christ! All this is very clear from a reading of 2 Corinthians Chapters 10 and 11, where Paul ends up declaring, *"such men are false apostles, deceitful workmen, masquerading as apostles of Christ"* (11:13).

And did you notice Paul's terminology in that last verse, *"deceitful workmen."* This parallels and confirms our use of the term, *"evil workers."*

Sombre, isn't it? And it brings to mind the Lord's fearful words, *"Many will say to me on that day, 'Lord, Lord, did we not prophesy in your name, and in your name drive out demons and perform many miracles?' Then I will tell them plainly, 'I never knew you. Away from me, you evildoers!'"* (Matthew 7:22-23)

The Final Day

There is a day coming that will try by fire the works of every one of us. When the Bible speaks of the foolish and the wise, it's not necessarily talking about the saved and the unsaved. It is just as much speaking about believers wise and foolish. When it refers to the righteous and the wicked, it is frequently about the righteous and wicked as found in church life. The righteous and the wicked often sit alongside each other in churches. Paul tells us that *"the fire will test the quality of each man's work"* (1 Corinthians 3:13), and for some, their works, so often paraded as 'spiritual works,' will be burned up as fleshly.

Think again about Proverbs 11:9. What if you happen to be the neighbour that is being destroyed by the mouth of the godless? How is it that some other Christian, by godless speech, can destroy you? Amongst other things, such as criticism, holding judgements, and jealousy (all of which by nature project witchcraft), it can and does happen when they persist in laying selfish claims on the city in which you live. These claims will be at work against all other genuine works of Christ.

Need more proof? Another scriptural witness? Here's Paul on the subject: *'The entire law is summed up in a single command: "Love your neighbor as yourself." If you keep on biting and devouring each other, watch out or you will be destroyed by each other'* (Galatians 5:14-15).

What can you do about this? Remember, Solomon adds, *"but through knowledge the righteous escape"* (v9). Here you are being instructed with some knowledge. Escape by praying out of an opposite spirit. Do something in your daily prayers to release your city. Relinquish your own claims and, whilst fully forgiving others for their sins against you, cut off their claims and start believing that God will fulfill His promises for your city. But you will need to persist.

The one referred to in Proverbs 11:12, who *"derides their neighbor"* because he/she *"has no sense,"* is the same person in verse 9 who destroys his *"neighbour"* with his *"mouth"* – but in contrast, the *"righteous"* is that person of *"understanding"* who *"holds their tongue."* The pastor and the church that think little of other churches do, in fact, *"deride"* them, and the Bible says these persons lack judgement, and this behaviour is that of *"the wicked."*

The Way of the Upright

For our encouragement Solomon includes this observation, as well as the warning: *"Through the blessing of the upright a city is exalted, but by the mouth of the wicked it is destroyed"* (v11).

We can pursue the course of the *"upright,"* that our city might have our *"blessing"* and become *"exalted,"* rather than allowing it to continue to be infected (and the work of God *"destroyed"*) by the *"mouth of the wicked."* We will all need to relinquish our claims.

Your claims might be righteous, they may have been just, you might be entitled to them, and they may come from a pure heart. It doesn't matter; we don't need to make claims, for we can believe God in better ways.

There are many other ways: the way of *love*; the way of *consideration*; the way of *humility*; the way of *submission*.

We must remember: we are here for the sake of other people. We ought not be thinking they are here for us, but rather commit ourselves to the heart-values that Christ and His apostles taught us to follow. I like to say; "We are here to make other people successful!" When we have that grace established in our hearts, then are we enabled to trust God to give us our *inheritance*, and make us a *fruitful* people.

This Calls for Prayer

All of us have beliefs, and we try to have right beliefs. But the attitudes of our hearts rise and fall, and probably there have been years in which we have carried many judgements concerning other Christians, and other churches. But it's time to let it all go. Let us ask the Lord to forgive us personally and as a people for every judgement, all criticism, any superiority, and for unrighteous beliefs that we hold – any belief that we are better, or that others are not so good. These beliefs are too numerous really, but let us ask the Lord to cleanse our hearts today.

First, a Prayer for Cleansing

"Father, I ask in the name of our Lord Jesus for your forgiveness today, for myself and for all your people, for the unrighteous beliefs that have been in our hearts. Forgive us for those attitudes and judgements we have held concerning ourselves and other believers that have made it so impossible for us to be knit together with others. I ask that you would make us a people able to be joined with others. Take from my heart this disparate condition which, in the name of the Lord Jesus, I reject. I renounce and repent of every fleshly belief I've held concerning myself or others. Father, I ask for the cleansing of my heart and mind, and I ask for all my people this same cleansing, in Jesus' name."

Second, a Prayer to Relinquish Claims

Now let us relinquish the claims. Remember that when you claim things, you are making claims that other people 'have to live under.' We can relinquish all of that. And we can trust the Lord for his mercies.

In this prayer we must take four steps:-
Firstly, we simply relinquish all our claims on our city.
Secondly, we'll pray for the city to prosper and for the city to be free.
Thirdly, we must pray to bless the church of Jesus Christ in the city.
Fourthly, we end with prayer for the Lord to give us our inheritance.

"Father, today in the name of our Lord Jesus we relinquish our claims upon the city and hand it all over to you. We declare that the city belongs to Jesus Christ. It is the Lord's city, and I ask, O Lord, for freedom for this city. I ask that by your grace and power you would cause this city to prosper. And I ask that you would prosper the whole Body of Christ in the city. I pray that you would knit together all the parts of the Body, that the church of this city would be whole and would become one. Father, we pray also that you would grant us our inheritance in this city. I thank you, for you do delight in giving a goodly portion to your people. We make ourselves available to you through submission, and we seek humility. Make us now a considerate people, an understanding people, a wise people. I ask that you would invest in us the wisdom of heaven. For these things we pray, in Jesus' name."

My Prayer for You

Now let me pray for you, to bless you, and to then command the blessings of peace and prosperity over you. Begin to believe that this blessing is yours.

"Father, I thank you for the lives of those sharing this prayer with me; and I take hold of your blessing for them, and declare it is theirs today, along with the peace of the Lord Jesus. I place that blessing on their mind, their heart, their home, and their family.

"Now, in the name of the Lord Jesus, I declare you to be blessed of the Lord, and chosen of God. May the Lord be pleased to prosper you. May His prosperity pursue you and overtake you. The Lord provide for you, the Lord enrich you, and the Lord strengthen and bless the work of your hands.

"The Lord grant you grace and favour. May His goodness rest upon you and good things come to your house. The Lord grant you strength and length of life; many days, and good days. The Lord grant you vigour in the body, and clarity of mind.

"The Lord bless all your relationships. The Lord bless your marriage, the Lord bless your children, and your children's children, and all that are to come. And may the Lord build you up in wisdom and understanding and in the fear of the Lord, and make you a great and a prosperous people. The Lord increase you, and show you favour, and heap up mighty blessings upon you.

"In the mighty name of Jesus I release you into the freedom of Christ and into the prosperity of the gospel. The Lord give you power in prayer, and great grace by which to win souls, for he who is wise wins souls. The Lord grant you this wisdom. And now, the spirit of prayer rise up in you so that by day and by night you walk in the fellowship of God. May your prayers be heard in heaven and all your prayers be answered. May the Lord pour out blessing on the earth because of you, and grant you a great posterity.

"In the name of the Lord Jesus I declare you are blessed! May the Lord bless your coming in and going out, the Lord prosper you in all you do, and may your children be filled with peace. Your children will rise up and call you blessed. May the Lord make your children mighty in the land, for this is the Lord's promise.

"And so may the Lord favour you, help you, strengthen you, and keep you until the day He comes for His own. Our Father, we thank you in Jesus' name. Amen."

CHAPTER SEVEN

The Church as One

*"My purpose is that they may be... united in love,
so that they may have the full riches of complete understanding,
in order that they may know the mystery of God, namely, Christ"*
(Colossians 2:2)

The apostle Paul wrote to the Colossians commending them, saying how delighted he was to see how *"orderly"*[1] they were. But he was not actually present – he was *"in the Spirit,"*[2] as John was on Patmos, and rejoicing at what he could see of the spirit realm around them.

Yet we must acknowledge the problem, highlighted by the last two chapters, of just how disorderly things are for us in our cities. I am, of course, referring to spiritual things being very much out of order. What I have been calling the 'spirit realm,' the Bible calls the *"heavenly realms."*[3] Under the fractured life of institutionalised, denominational Christianity, along with its sectarian spirit and strong vested interests, not to mention the selfish ambition and envy of individual ministers, and the fleshly basis upon which so much is done, our cities are far from 'orderly.'

---

1 Colossians 2:5
2 Revelation 1:10
3 Ephesians 3:10, 6:12

I hope we can all now see the need for city elderships. More than anything else, city elderships are needed to address the disorder of spiritual and practical church life. It is time to rebuild our cities. And at this time, there is an apostolic call of Christ to do so, in the spirit of Isaiah 58:12, *"Your people will rebuild the ancient ruins and will raise up the age-old foundations; you will be called Repairer of Broken Walls, Restorer of Streets with Dwellings."*

We must come to see that simply electing a group of key believers within a local fellowship, no matter how Godly they are, and calling them elders, does not equate with biblical eldership. Though many churches have done things that way for a long time, the Lord is now about to restore biblical eldership.

Surely, if we have any respect for the Scriptures, and any fear of God at all, we must be willing to see that the eldership of the future will be a leadership over the whole church of the whole city, made up from qualified fivefold ministers. We can still build leadership teams appropriate for our churches without calling people elders who are not elders, while at the same time opening up our hearts for a future eldership that represents Christ to be built in our cities and towns by the Spirit of God.

At Peace we made a decision in the year 2000 that from that time no-one but fivefold ministers could be considered elders in the New Testament sense. We have never regretted that decision, and in the period since have made very good progress in the things of the Spirit, as well as in our ministry goals.

The reformation of the church calls for a clear understanding and activation of some very basic biblical concepts. In any given locality (i.e. in any city, town, or region), the church should be recognisably *one body*, with a *common leadership* which the New Testament calls *elders*. Every leader should walk in accountable relationships, and the elders and every ministry should be under apostolic covering. Apostles and prophets should be functioning as foundational ministries of the church.

And when a larger, all-in leadership meeting is needed, such as the Jerusalem Council, it is the *apostles and elders* gathered together.[4]

The implications of these concepts are very far-reaching. If we believe these biblical truths, this does call for a major overhaul of church structure, a complete reformation to restore the apostolic wineskin of the church.

The Church is One

There is not a church or denomination anywhere in the world that does not teach the unity of the church, i.e. that the church is one Body, and that we all belong to the whole Body of Christ. Unfortunately, for much of the church, this is only a theory. The way we live, and the way most of the church actually functions, is quite different.

The Body of Christ, as we have known it, is a far cry from being one Body in any practical, recognisable way, although we do see that progress is being made — reform is under way. Some might argue that the unity of the Body of Christ is spiritual, mystical, and eternal; that the truth of unity is not necessarily measured outwardly. Whilst there is some truth in that, and on earth there will always be tares amongst the wheat and challenges to the unity of the church, nevertheless an outward unity is required by Holy Scripture. We are to make every effort, to work hard in fact, to maintain the *"unity of the spirit"* in the church (Ephesians 4:3), *"until,"* we are assured, we all come to the *"unity of the faith"* (Ephesians 4:13). Divisive 'believers' are to be removed and ostracised by all believers if they do not heed suitable warnings (Titus 3:10, 1:10-11,13). The right spirit by which this is to be done is covered by Paul in 2 Thessalonians 3:14-15.

It is obvious from the prayers of our Lord Jesus that the unity of the church is meant to be <u>outward, visible, practical, recognisable, and effective</u>. Jesus prayed for us, His future disciples, *"that all of them may be one, father, just as you are in*

---

4 Acts 15:2, 6.

me and I am in you... so that the world may believe that you have sent me." He further prayed, *"that they may be one as we are one: I in them and you in me. May they be brought to complete unity to let the world know that you sent me and have loved them"* (John 17:21-23). The unity called for is comparable to the unity of the Father and the Son, described by Jesus as *"complete unity"* – one which is so visible and recognisable that the world sees it, and so effective that the world believes the Word of God.

You know very well that we do not have this oneness, except perhaps in a few rare places. Something must change, and the Spirit of God is calling for the change. But it begins with us, with a change of our hearts and our values. We must develop understanding. We must take seriously what Scripture tells us about the nature of the Body of Christ. We must be prepared to obey. We must be prepared to put aside some things we have previously clung to, and yield in submission to doing things God's way.

This unity is meant to be a *real* and *practical* unity, no more just a theory. We must be a people devoted to each other from the heart (Romans 12:10, 1 Peter 1:22), sharing a true love and acceptance of one another (Romans 15:7), and enjoying a true common unity, which is 'community' (Acts 2:44). We are meant to stand together as one man (Philippians 1:27), and to think with one mind and speak with one voice (Acts 4:32, Romans 15:5-6). In any given community the church is meant to have a solidarity of witness which is in total unity and harmony.

When I read the following Scripture I hear the cry of the Holy Spirit. *"There is one body and one Spirit — just as you were called to one hope when you were called — one Lord, one faith, one baptism; one God and Father of all, who is over all and through all and in all"* (Ephesians 4:4-6). What I hear the Spirit cry is, "One body! — *One body! — **One body! —** **ONE BODY!**"* This is because there is only one Jesus, there is but one Holy Spirit, there is just one baptism, there is one God alone, and the household of God is the **one and only** household of God.

We must have our eyes opened, and allow the truth of God's word to actually grip our hearts. We can no longer live for ourselves, self-serving in our own spiritual worlds where our own influence and our own way rules supreme. Rather, we must recognise the clear implications of these Scriptures. The Body of Jesus is one household, one family, and over this family God has ordained a method of leadership whereby all believers can look to a common leadership – that of the apostles and elders. This form of leadership does not require an institution, so there is no talk here of amalgamating denominations. Rather, we are trying to escape from the institutionalisation of Christianity.

For years I have noticed something very, very strange. In towns, cities, and rural communities right across the nation, there are Christian believers who never, or rarely, speak to each other, who never attend the same meetings or worship gatherings, who never pray together, and who never share their vision, their goals, or their faith with each other. Yet they live in the same community! And in some cases they live in the same street! What is more strange is that very often they will have near identical prayer goals and vision for their community. What keeps them apart is *institutionalised* Christianity — they happen to belong to a different denomination, or a different movement, from each other. They act as total strangers, they are virtually foreigners, and have been alienated from each other – by 'religion.'

We find the same strange phenomena occurring with ministers of the gospel. Even in small towns there are ministers who know of each other, but do not communicate or share in any meaningful way, yet they claim to have the same call to follow the same Christ, and to believe the same Bible. When you get to know them they will often have the same goals for the community. They will be praying for the lost to be saved, and for the Spirit of revival to come upon their town or city. There will be several others in town each leading their own small flock in prayer for the community to be saved and for the Holy Spirit to move amongst them, yet they will never meet with them, and they never actively seek a way for the Body to be whole.

Does this not seem strange to you? That born-again, spirit-filled believers who have the same beliefs, pray the same prayers, and believe in the unity of the church, are never given the opportunity *by their leaders* to connect and cooperate in any meaningful way. And this despite what the New Testament instructs.

Is there an explanation for this strange and grotesque peculiarity that occurs in much of the Christian world? There are two observations that could be made, both of which I believe to be true.

One is that there is upon the leaders of the church a mindset, a denominational and institutional paradigm. It is the leaders and the denominational structure that is at fault — the shepherds have erected fences that keep the sheep apart. In my experience the problem is never that the sheep are unwilling to mix. The leaders of the church will need to see things differently, or God will raise other leaders before too long.

The second observation is that a religious spirit combines with fallen human nature to keep much of Christianity blind to all of this. A spiritual veil has been over our hearts, hindering us. A deceiving spirit of division has taken advantage and has worked to maintain a separation that is contrary to the will of God. And the hearts of men have allowed this in the course of the church's history.

However, this is a new day, and here is the Scripture for today!

"Consequently, you are no longer foreigners and aliens, but fellow citizens with God's people and members of God's household, built on the foundation of the apostles and prophets, with Christ Jesus himself as the chief cornerstone. In him the whole building is joined together and rises to become a holy temple in the Lord. And in him you too are being built together to become a dwelling in which God lives by his Spirit" (Ephesians 2:19-22).

No longer foreigners! No longer strangers or aliens! Why? Because you are fellow citizens and members of one household! What is the key here? Apostles and prophets! — as you can see from the text.

The word *'built'* is here used twice. To obtain the desired result described in verses 21-22, these believers are firstly *'built on'* the foundation that is provided by apostles and prophets, and then they can be *'built together'*. This brings the most dramatic result of all — they become a dwelling (a house) in which God lives by His Spirit.

If we are not careful, we will miss the amazing significance of the final verse (22), because we are already familiar with the idea of the previous verse (21). For years and years we have all been taught that the unity of the church is eternal and mystical, and we were not encouraged to have great hope for anything in this world beyond perhaps unity in the local congregation or the denomination. We were told, correctly, that all the believers of all ages who were in relationship with Jesus were God's household, and that God was building an eternal temple, in which we were all living stones . That is true, precisely what we are to believe, and Ephesians 2:21 (above) describes this for our faith.

But the following verse is not speaking of the same thing. Verses 21 and 22 sound similar, but they are not saying the same thing in different ways. First Paul speaks of the whole building, and then he speaks of a *local* building. Every one of us, in our daily walk with others, is meant to be *'built'* into a body that will be a house for God to live in by His Spirit, *in our city*. This *'dwelling'* is meant to be built as part of our present, local experience of Christ, in every place where there is a church.

Here we must make an all-important, climactic decision. In any given geographical locality, there can be only one church. There is only one Body; it is *the* church. We must allow this truth to change our attitudes, our values, our prayers, and our goals.

I am not proposing that there should be a merger of denominations so that we have just one denomination — that is not the church unity we are speaking of. To do that is to assume the church is an institution, which it never is. Rather, we are talking of the restoration of the apostolic church, where unity is based on actual relationships, values, love, and devotion under the authority of apostles and the leadership of elders. Of this the church fathers confessed this creed, "We believe in one, holy, catholic *(universal)*, and apostolic church."[5]

One day in prayer I had a vision. I could see through the office wall into the auditorium, and it was as if I was seeing all the people worshiping on Sunday. And these were great people, prayerful, faithful Christians. I could see them singing and praying, when I heard the Lord speak, "The reason many believers experience sickness, and often struggle to receive answers to prayer, is because they do not pray for the unity of the church."

Could this statement really be true? As I weighed it up, I realised this was indeed a profound truth. Every believer is a dynamic part of the whole Body of Christ. We are each connected to all other believers, not in theory but with actual spiritual power, and the health and well-being of the whole Body affects us personally. If we are careless and neglectful in our hearts toward the Body of Christ, that carelessness and

5 The Nicene Creed.

neglect affects us. If we have no care for the health of the Body of Christ, our prayers for our own selves and families, and our own congregations, have been rendered powerless by our attitude. This is the same spiritual dynamic at work as that concerning a man's prayers if he does not honour his wife (1 Peter 3:7).

Not only that, but if we are critical or disparaging of other parts of the Body, we are cursing ourselves. You cannot curse a part without cursing the whole. You who curse are a living part of what you have cursed. This is why Paul wrote to the Corinthians, struggling as they were with a problem of division, these startling words, *"For anyone who eats and drinks without recognizing the body of the Lord eats and drinks judgment on himself. That is why many among you are weak and sick, and a number of you have fallen asleep. But if we judged ourselves, we would not come under judgment"* (1 Corinthians 11:29-32).

The weakness referred to here is spiritual weakness, the sickness is physical, and some of them had died prematurely. This is a genuine judgement of sin in the church (the sin was that of wrong attitudes to the Body of Christ), and as a result both spiritual and physical weaknesses and sicknesses abound. Yet Paul had said that the Corinthian church came behind in no gift (1 Corinthians 1:7). Here was a church that had the gifts of the Spirit in abundance (gifts such as discerning of spirits, prophecy, words of knowledge, and healing too), yet could not see the answers to their own problems, because they were under judgement. And the root cause of that judgement? Their attitude to one another — they did not recognise others as Christ!

This is no different to what many believers do today. Very few recognise the need to pray for the unity of the Body of Christ as a pressing priority for prayer. No wonder weakness abounds. But when we pray blessing upon the Body of Christ, such as health, vigour, wisdom, progress in the faith, revelation of Christ, possessing inheritance, etc. – and pray for the growth and success of other churches – we are able to receive these blessings for ourselves. The unity of the Body must be the great goal of our prayers, our faith, and our active obedience.

These conclusions about unity raise the question of leadership. If the Body is whole, one, a unit, and if it is to be so in some honest, practical, and visible way, then there must *also* be unity of *leadership*. The Bible does indeed provide such a model for the leadership of the church, and it is an apostolic model, as we shall see. This is where city eldership comes in.

A Common Leadership for the One Church

The first thing one should notice about the church in the New Testament is that it is strikingly different to the church as we know it today; in any given city or locality there was only one church. Paul's epistles were written to churches at Corinth or Ephesus, for example, which were cities; or to Galatia, which was a region. The point is that wherever there were Christians, there was but one church – and these churches all accepted each other as *the* church.

The seven letters of Jesus recorded in The Book of Revelation, chapters 2 and 3, are each written to a single church, and each was the church of a whole city. Nowhere in the New Testament do we find anything that allows for any other option but one church in one locality. Anything else is a division of the Body.

The second thing we notice about the church of the New Testament is that it had an amazingly diverse leadership, yet one that remained bound together in love as part of one whole. This remained so despite difficult issues that had to be worked through by the early church. Even when there were personal differences, there is no sense that this produced a divergent leadership (compare Acts 15:39 with Colossians 4:10, and Galatians 2:11 with 2 Peter 3:15).

The apostolic church had a single, identifiable, authoritative, relational leadership structure. It was not every man for himself;

each knew they belonged to each other in the fear of the Lord, and there was an ultimate accountability to the apostles, as well as a submission to the instruction of those apostles.

In the biblical revelation, the leadership of the apostolic church recognised one another, walked in mutual submission and respect toward each another, and worked together knowing they shared an eternal relationship in the covenant that God had made with us in Christ. There was a spiritual 'fabric' that linked the fivefold ministry of the church in the anointings of Christ, and they knew it. This is what must again be found amongst us, and we will do so, because in these days God is giving His people a new heart. The anointing for leadership in these days is to give Jesus the church as He wants it.

Eldership as seen in the New Testament

Where the *Acts of the Apostles* begins its narrative, the only recognisable ministry and the only position of any official status in the church is that of the apostles. But before long there were deacons, evangelists, prophets, and teachers. Then, at the end of Chapter 11, we find the first reference to an *eldership* in the church: *"During this time some prophets came down from Jerusalem to Antioch. One of them, named Agabus, stood up and through the Spirit predicted that a severe famine would spread over the entire Roman world. (This happened during the reign of Claudius.) The disciples, each according to his ability, decided to provide help for the brothers living in Judea. This they did, sending their gift to the elders by Barnabas and Saul"* (Acts 11:27-30).

From this we understand that the church in Jerusalem had been under the leadership of an eldership from an early time. As we read on, we learn that *"Paul and Barnabas appointed elders for them in each church and, with prayer and fasting, committed them to the Lord."* (Acts 14:23) Wherever apostles established churches, sooner or later they appointed elders. But in keeping with what we learned above about the nature of the apostolic church (i.e. one church in one locality), the elders appointed were the spiritual leaders for the whole city or the whole region.

This Paul confirms when he wrote to Titus; *"The reason I left you in Crete was that you might straighten out what was left unfinished and appoint elders in every town, as I directed you"* (Titus 1:5-6).

Chapter 15 of Acts records the fascinating account of the events surrounding the 'Jerusalem Council', a special meeting of the senior leadership of the church, called to make an authoritative decision concerning what was to be required of Gentiles who became believers. In that chapter there is a recurring phrase, shown in the following quotations:

> *"So Paul and Barnabas were appointed, along with some other believers, to go up to Jerusalem to see **the apostles and elders** about this question."* (Acts 15:2)

> *"When they came to Jerusalem, they were welcomed by the church and **the apostles and elders.**"* (Acts 15:4)

> ***"The apostles and elders** met to consider this question."* (Acts 15:6)

> *"Then **the apostles and elders**, with the whole church, decided to choose some of their own men and send them to Antioch with Paul and Barnabas."* (Acts 15:22)

> *"With them they sent the following letter: **The apostles and elders**, your brothers, To the Gentile believers in Antioch, Syria and Cilicia: Greetings. We have heard that some went out from us without our authorization and disturbed you."* (Acts 15:23-24)

Here we see that the apostles were a part of the eldership of the church, yet at the same time distinct from it. These apostles worked as one with the other elders, but nevertheless held an authority as apostles that was not dissipated within the workings of this group of leaders. This is even more pronounced when we observe that whilst everyone present had much to contribute in debate (Acts 15:7), and Peter made a final authoritative appeal, in the end the leader of the Jerusalem church, James, made a final judgement on the matter (Acts 15:13,19). This was not democracy at work, but community.

We saw earlier, in Chapter 4, that the eldership is made up of apostles, prophets, and teachers (these teachers are the *"pastors and teachers"* of Ephesians 4:11, which probably refers to a combination role, rather than separate ones.) The Bible provides a model of such an eldership at work: *'In the church at Antioch there were prophets and teachers: Barnabas, Simeon called Niger, Lucius of Cyrene, Manaen (who had been brought up with Herod the tetrarch) and Saul. While they were worshiping the Lord and fasting, the Holy Spirit said, "Set apart for me Barnabas and Saul for the work to which I have called them." So after they had fasted and prayed, they placed their hands on them and sent them off'* (Acts 13:1-3). Here the eldership was specifically comprised of prophets and teachers, who had been working together in the leadership of that city for some time. It is evident from other Scripture that Barnabas was a prophet and Paul a teacher. After some time in the eldership, revelation came that called them to other work, and so they were released into their apostolic mission.

We are told in verse 2 that they were together *"worshipping the Lord and fasting."* That's what elders are supposed to do: meet together, worship together, love each other deeply from the heart, serve one another, and serve the church and the city together. They were one in leading and guarding the church and the city. And God speaks to them. This is where they will often hear God.

We do not have evidence to show that evangelists are normally in the eldership. This does not necessarily exclude them, since they are ministers of Christ with a fivefold ascension anointing. Still, the practicality of the matter is that the ministry of an evangelist is not for the purpose of the pastoral care of the church, which is the primary purpose of the eldership. The eldership appointment is especially one for watching over the flock of a particular locality (Acts 20:28, 1 Peter 5:1-4). An evangelist would not necessarily be gifted for, or called to this role.

Of special note is that not every fivefold minister of a given city can be in the eldership. If this were so, there would be no need for Paul's list of qualifications for such leaders, as sent to Timothy and Titus. Neither, in that case, would Paul advise Timothy that "if anyone aspires to the office of overseer, he desires a noble task" (1 Timothy 3:1). And it so happens that there are believers who are called to the fivefold ministry, and who are spiritually gifted and functioning in ministry, but who are totally unsuitable for the eldership and the covering because of character issues. They may be gifted in accordance with their faith and their call, and have built or are attempting to build ministries, but simply do not qualify for the eldership. Others are unsuitable because they are still maturing, or for other practical reasons.

If we would bring the church into the fullness of Christ,[6] following the principles of the revelation of the New Testament, and if we wish to overcome the problem of the great void of leadership at the city-wide level which leaves the Body of Christ vulnerable and immature, we must act and do something about restoring city elderships – and restoring apostolic covering to those elderships.

City Eldership: How Do We Get There?

Firstly, we have a difficulty: elders in the New Testament were only ever appointed by the apostles, and whilst necessity may require other methods at times, such as, in the absence of apostles, existing elders and ministers agreeing amongst

6 Ephesians 4:13

themselves, this is the only *biblical* model we have. For example: *"Paul and Barnabas appointed elders for them in each church and, with prayer and fasting, committed them to the Lord"* (Acts 14:23), and *"The reason I left you in Crete was that you might straighten out what was left unfinished and appoint elders in every town, as I directed you"* (Titus 1:5).

Our problem is that the apostolic ministry is still being restored, we see only the early part of a longer process, and it is as yet hardly understood by much of the church. Neither is anything like the proper nature of apostolic authority yet restored to apostles as leaders of the church, although it will come. We are at the stage, rather, of building relationships of trust, love, and accountability.

We need to start building elderships, but it cannot be that some outsider to a city, even if greatly gifted as an apostle, can unilaterally appoint elders. For one, most local church leaders cannot and should not accept this. I would say, as an observation of New Testament church life and apostolic ministry, that the apostles of the New Testament, such as Paul and Titus named above, never did appoint elders unilaterally.

They had the authority to lay hands on elders, yes, but did so within a rich community context. These apostles were intimate with the churches, lived among them, and had long-established relationships with the believers and all the leaders. They not only knew them well, they walked with them, and would never have appointed elders as leaders without much consultation and agreement, or without knowing intimately both those appointed and those who would work closely with them. In other words, it came out of the apostles being part of the community life of the local church.[7]

7 For a greater discussion of apostolic authority, and of what authority apostles do not have, see my book, *The Apostolic Revelation*. I also explain the two 'rules of thumb' for the exercise of spiritual authority: No authority without relationship, and No authority without responsibility.

City eldership can only be built as a work of the Spirit of God. Christ said He would build the church (Matthew 16:18). But the Holy Spirit does give us wisdom, revealing His plans and purpose so that we may cooperate with Him, because we are co-labourers in building the house of God (Psalm 127:1, 1 Corinthians 3:10).

There are certain things essential to achieving this purpose. We must build *relationships*, change *values*, *pray earnestly* for God to build the city eldership and unity of the Body, and *yield,* i.e. *allow* the Holy Spirit to make changes and bring about these results.

Firstly, Build Relationships

The only way forward is with what comes from heart relationship. In every place, real men and women of God must find each other, and begin to walk and talk together. They are personally the ministry of Christ, not the institution to which they belong. They must begin to accept each other personally, despite any initial differences. The Body will be built by leaders in relationship, whose hearts will be knit together like David and Jonathan (1 Samuel 18:1-4), and who will bring the people of the whole church into a one-heart, one-mind relationship (Acts 4:32). Only leaders of genuine spiritual integrity are capable of these personal and rich relationships.

The entire new wineskin of the church will be based on relationships that are personal rather than formal and institutional. Until now, very little genuine relationship of a personal nature has existed between most pastors in any given area. Despite a doctrine that said they were brothers, in practice they were competitors, and well outside each other's circle of friends. Though ministers of the gospel, living in and appointed to the same location, they were strangers to one another.

Relationship has to be built, but cannot be built using

meetings that have a business agenda. We've all tried it, and it doesn't work. Relationship has to be based on friendship and genuine love. The only way to build friendship is to spend time together with no other purpose than that. When we get to know others well as friends, we come to love them. And when we love them, we come to trust them. This is the only basis for partnership in ministry.

If you think my emphasis on personal, loving, friendship is inaccurate, consider what may be the most common form of address and endearment we find in the New Testament epistles. Paul, Peter, John, Jude, and the writer to the Hebrews all address their people as *'agapetos'*, which is, beloved. This is the same form of address the Father uses for Jesus. It is translated in various versions as *"dearly beloved,"* and *"dear brothers,"* and in the NIV as *"friends"* or *"dear friends."* Jude in his short letter uses this expression three times, the apostle John uses it six times in his first epistle, Peter uses it twice in his first epistle and four times in his second, and Paul uses it in three epistles. This surely is a significant, not a casual, use of language.

Some Experiences in Relationship Building

I mentioned earlier that Rockhampton was historically a spiritually divided city – not divided in the obvious sense of opposition, bitterness, or criticism between churches (not in living memory, anyway, except in some individual cases). Instead, in this city the churches have, generally, simply gone their own way. They focused on their own work and their own needs, and saw no need for anything more.

After my first year as the pastor at Peace, I noticed a curiosity — in the course of that whole year there had been no occasion to meet with other ministers. I had not become familiar with even one other pastor in the city, and none had contacted me. I made enquiries, and was informed that there had not been a meeting of any ministers' fraternal in Rockhampton for over 20 years. No trouble was evident, simply apathy. This was a yawning chasm of division, which outwardly appeared simply as indifference.

Early in my second year I wrote to all the pastors and the bishops. I proposed that every month we have lunch together — no agenda, no chairman, no secretary, no minutes, no treasurer, no business except having lunch and talking. This continued for six years with mixed results. The ministers of the older historic traditional churches were generally regular attenders, but the pastors of evangelical and Pentecostal denominations were almost all conspicuous by their absence. Most of the ones who claimed to believe and obey the Bible more, and love Christ the most passionately, were the least moved (at that time, not now) by any appeal to develop relationship with others. The main reason given was that it was a waste of time, because nothing would change.

This did not become a great unity movement in the city, although I was glad to develop friendship and cooperation with others whom I came to love. The very institutional and structural nature of the churches represented, combined with the underlying curses and spiritual strongholds of the city, prevented anything exceptional developing at that point.

There was one shaft of light that appeared for a time, however. In the neighbourhood where Peace was located were four other churches, namely Anglican, Catholic, Lutheran, and Uniting churches. These four were traditional, while Peace was, call us what you will, contemporary/ charismatic/ Pentecostal/ prophetic etc., but something very interesting eventuated amongst us.

Because of those monthly lunch meetings, the Catholic priest felt close enough to us, his neighbours, to invite us to his house on Friday afternoons, where we would share coffee and cake, and talk. At the time the Catholic Church was working through a group programme called 'Renew', and he invited us to participate in some of those exercises. All of this helped develop an acceptance, and some trust. Soon we began having regular combined church services. Even though our Sunday worship at Peace was wonderful, and things seemed a bit more 'contained' when meeting with the others, I was surprised that some of the best and sweetest experiences of God we had during that period were actually when we met together with these other churches.

From this experience I discovered a power dynamic. When leaders enjoy personal relationship with one another, with affection and acceptance, then there is power and divine presence when their people meet. This was vastly different from the usual 'ecumenical' services I had attended previously. Those had brought together various parts of the Body but, by comparison, lacked power and anointing, because there was not any sense of personal relationship between the leaders.

Unfortunately, as always in the way of the institutional church, all four of these pastors were relocated, and the fellowship ceased to exist. Then some years went by when suddenly, after what appeared a void of relationships, there came something sovereign, wonderful, and fruitful — real relationship with other ministry leaders. God brought three men, each of different movements or denominations, together for friendship and intimacy and trust. We had not previously had any relationship, and very little contact with each other.

I cannot remember what changed, or how it happened, or who initiated it, but two other ministers and I began finding ourselves meeting every week. It was quickly apparent that this was the most important event of our week, and we devoted fully half a day — just to talk. We talked for hours, about anything and everything, but especially about Christ, and grace, and our expectations and hopes. We shared about our families, our experiences, and our approach to ministry and preaching. Our acceptance of each other grew into love and trust. Our lives became enriched and our hearts knitted, and we cared about each other's success. All the while we talked, we were, without planning anything, sharing and exploring our values, until we discovered how much we held in common. We were of one heart, and had a remarkably similar vision for the work of God.

Then our wives began to get together, and their love and acceptance of each other was even greater than our own. Fellows are slow — it was through our women that we discovered more about how the men saw each other, and how we saw the future of the relationship and the church of the city. Here was a deep desire for God to do with the church whatever He wanted, and to not hold back from giving God whatever He asked of us.

One day in April 2001, in prayer, there was a great breakthrough in defeating a major principality, a spirit of division that had been in the city for a long time. This opened the way for a number of wonderful developments. Within two months we began having combined church services, and something better was happening in the hearts of our people. Now the people of one church would think of the members of the other as belonging to them. They were all our people. I visited an elderly woman who had attended my church for years and loved me, but who was now having difficulty travelling to our meetings. She lived opposite one of those churches. I said to her, "These are good people, and they are our family. If you worship with them, you are worshipping with us." She has been there ever since.

Gone was the distance that was between us, and gone the spirit of competition. Once, one of those pastors was to be away. He instructed his youth leader that if he had any problems while he was away, he was to come and see one of us and talk to us about it. That is trust.

In that trust is the inner peace that comes from knowing there is but one church in the city, and that your brothers will guard your place and your work in it.

That was some years ago, but there are even better things

getting underway right now, although these are still early days in the new relationships that are forming. There is much yet to be built by the Holy Spirit here. In the city are other ministers of Christ, and somehow the Holy Spirit will build the more extensive fellowship and trust in the coming days, and, we pray and trust, will build an eldership over the city.

At Peace, our people are actively praying for God to build the unity of the Body and establish the eldership of the city, and our hearts are ready to grow in relationship with those leaders. Last Sunday I instructed our people to not just pray in a general way for the unity of the church, but to pray very specifically to bless and lift up every individual minister they knew, and their churches.

But there will be no true eldership, there *cannot be* a biblical eldership, without the elders being in personal, committed, trusting, heart relationship with each other. Those who desire the *"noble task"*[8] of serving as elders should look, in the first instance, for such relationships, and the people of God should pray for them to be established. There is great authority and power in the spiritual covering as a result of such relationships.

Secondly, Change Values

Whenever we need to make changes in church life, we must remember the crucial maxim, **"don't change structures until you change values."** In other words, we must see that the people we work with *understand* things differently before we ask them to *do* things differently. Even when it is the will of God for change to take place, we will get more cooperation when people understand through having a proper set of values.

We always function according to what we really believe, whether we are conscious of it or not. While ever pastors and leaders hold only the traditional values, or concepts, of either their denominational or their 'independent' background, there will be little change. We must insist that church leaders have an

---

8 1 Timothy 3:1

open, believing heart to embrace what Scripture tells us about the Body of Christ, not what is demanded by church traditions, denominational vested interests, or the stronghold of the way things have simply been in their experience.

As more and more Christian leaders are motivated by Christ's passion for His church in accordance with biblical values, we will see a transformation take place in church life in community after community. This is a current work of the Holy Spirit being carried forward all over the world.

Thirdly, Earnest Prayer

There are many strongholds to be brought down, and many underlying curses to be broken, not only in towns and cities but also in churches. Satan has taken advantage on many past occasions to entrench traditions, divisions, and cultural attitudes, to resist and prevent the future unity of the church. Warfare prayer and supplication with tears is needed, not in an occasional manner, but as a devoted way of life by the many saints who have understanding. For many, intercession and sacrifice in vigilant spiritual warfare is to be a long-term lifestyle, until the church becomes mature (Isaiah 62: 6-7, Ephesians 4: 13-16).

Most of the things God has promised, and which are in the ministry visions of leaders, cannot be achieved without intercession. The greatest need of all, and our greatest opportunity, is to pray for the unity of the Body of Christ, and the restoration of apostles and New Testament eldership. More than anything, this will have a direct bearing on the health, well-being, and success of all Christians, their families, and their businesses, as well as the life and ministry of the church.

Fourthly, Allow the Holy Spirit to Have His Way

God wants to bring change, and He is asking for our cooperation. This will mean surrender in some areas where we thought we owned the ground. We must make room for others, and pastors will need to embrace the greater vision of the city.

All local ministries need to embrace the values and pursue the goal of becoming *"one in heart and mind"*[9] with the other leaders of the city, and with those who grow into the eldership role. There will be, in the Lord, an overall anointing for spiritual leadership of the city, and all who have ministry in the city will need to be in harmony with that anointing.

Every pastor will have to address, in their own hearts, the issue of independence, and of their 'rights', no matter how large their church. Christ's leaders will need to give each other their hearts. We are not called to be independent; we are called to be one. And the Holy Spirit is well able to make us one, if we will love the truth enough, with a pure heart that does not carry a 'private' agenda. This calls for the heart of integrity that is to be in the true shepherd.[10]

If the leaders of a city have right values, and clear understanding of what God wants, and where He is taking the church, then with perseverance, prayer, and surrendered hearts, Christ will build a city eldership for the church. Some cities have already made progress in this journey.

And we thank God, the Holy Spirit is moving the Body of Christ towards the spiritual maturity envisaged in Scripture.

Safeguarding the Eldership

But who guards the eldership, and watches over the spirit of it? Who guides their attitudes, relationships, spirituality, unity, and purity of biblical doctrine by providing a means of accountability and the input of spiritual fathering, with the genuine authority of Christ?

There is, providentially, a biblical provision. City elderships need to relate to apostles. This we will consider in the following chapter.

But What Were Our Prayers?

Before we move on, I am aware I haven't told you as yet

---

9 Acts 4:32
10 Psalm 78:72, Ezekiel 34:7-10, 22-24

what the prayers were that led to Australia's wettest 2-year season in recorded history. What kind of prayer caused the Lord to say, "As a result of these prayers, water will flow..." And it did, breaking the great drought, and putting huge flows over two years down the Murray/Darling River system to address Australia's biggest environmental nightmare, replenishing aquifers and healing the land. So much so that it caused the great floods of Dec 2011-Feb 2012.

You might remember, it began with me asking Lynda to seek the Lord with the question, **"What do we need to do to get the final breakthrough for the city."** And after waiting on the Lord over months, Lynda came back with His reply, which might not seem like an answer: **"The old eldership is resisting the new eldership."**

What did that mean? At first, I thought it was all about the old eldership of Peace, which had come into a time of division from 1996 to 1998, after which several of those elders left but were critical of us. It occurred to me that we had appointed them as elders, laid hands on them and given them authority in the church, but this authority over our church life had never been rescinded. This meant that any judgements they continued to hold were still powerfully active against us. So my first prayer, with other leaders, was to rescind the authority we had given them, which no longer applied, and was not eldership authority anyway.

But as I did so, I realised the city was *full* of "old elderships." Firstly, there would be a long history of leaders leaving other churches and carrying any of the following: criticism and judgements about the church they left, judgemental opinions and assumptions about other churches and pastors in the city, or critical opinions about the city itself. Any of these is a curse on the Body of Christ and on the city – especially from Christian leaders.

Secondly, there were many churches that had a current group

of elders, or a similar leadership team. Once again, the same components are often present as with those who have left. In addition, there is often present those exclusive belief systems that make us "disparate" – that we are better than others. So if a current group of leaders believe they are "the elders" of the "best" or "correct" expression of Christianity in the city, by default this is a great hindrance to the advance of the city, and obfuscates the work of God for us all.

So I began to pray, seeking a way to overcome all of that. But as I did, I realised there were many other "old elderships" in the city. The Masonic Lodge has such leaders, with deadly claims and exclusive attitudes. Then there is an aboriginal eldership, with its many claims. In addition, there is a civic leadership with such spiritual attachments, and some along the way promoted as "fathers of the city." Then there are all the cults, with their notoriously exclusive claims. It is, obviously, quite extensive and multi-layered. Once again, a simple word from the Lord turns out to be incredibly profound.

It was with these insights that Hazel and I began our long drives.

On the first trip, when we stood in the cities and towns we drove through, I exercised the authority of the Lord Jesus to rescind the false authority of all the old elderships, and prayed for the Lord to raise the new eldership for that town, establish His fivefold ministry in that place, and raise apostles and prophets for the Body of Christ. It all took 3-5 minutes.

On the second trip, when we prayed non-stop over eight days for every place we saw named on a signpost, we extended the prayers. Knowing by now the power of it, and the outcomes, we took all the prayer needs above, prayed a lot more thoroughly over them, and added in some previous knowledge. We added the binding of denominational spirits, and the cutting off of denominational claims and other fleshly claims, over each town and city. And the heavens opened.

There is something I need to make clear: some aspects of these prayers are beyond the authority of most believers, and this includes most who see themselves as intercessors. Whilst many parts of these prayers can be prayed by every responsible Christian, there are some specific needs here that can only be addressed by those with a specific Christ-given authority – I am referring in particular to rescinding false, assumed, authority of old elderships. This can only be done, in the main, by apostles who may have been given such authority, by city elderships if established, and perhaps by church fellowships functioning in one accord under anointed fivefold leadership when seeking to throw off spiritual bondage from themselves and their city.

This part of our prayers Hazel did not pray, even though she is highly experienced in prayer and quite gifted with prophetic discernment, and nor can just any Christian. She could intercede, and could bind spirits, cut off fleshly claims, and pray for Christ to raise great leaders and a true eldership, but to rescind false authority was beyond the grace she could exercise.

All Christians, no matter how new in the faith, can bind Satan and deal with spirits – although the outcomes will be dependent on their exercise of faith and their understanding of spiritual authority, which varies. But most will not have the kind of authority I refer to. It has to be given by the Lord, because this is not dealing with spirits (a general authority given to all believers by the Word of God), but is rather an exercise of authority over circumstances in which a spurious, fleshly, contrived, and 'religious,' authority has been established by man, and seen as 'official' by many. It takes a high level of Christ's delegated authority to effectively set this aside, and is one more reason why we do need apostles and city elderships – so that the Body of Christ may benefit by having a leadership that does exercise spiritual authority.

In every case, these prayers were dealing with the entrenched tradition and false religiosity attached to the Christian Church.

The state of our nations and cities really is affected negatively when, instead of being an apostolic people, with biblical government and order, and loving each other as Christ loved His disciples, we are instead very religious, and bound with vested selfish interest.

Thank God we can be free from all of this, and the 21st Century reformation of the church is underway.

CHAPTER EIGHT

The Authority We Need

*"For even if I boast somewhat freely
about the authority the Lord gave us for building you up
rather than pulling you down,
I will not be ashamed of it."*
(2 Corinthians 10:8)

*"Obey your leaders and submit to their authority.
They keep watch over you as men who must give an account.
Obey them so that their work will be a joy, not a burden,
for that would be of no advantage to you."*
(Hebrews 13:17)

There must be authority in the church, just as there must in education, business, the family home, and civil government. In the Old Testament, God always appointed key leaders for His people, and in the same way, in the New Testament Christ appointed apostles. Even the Lord Jesus Himself did not minister in this world except as a man under authority, a matter commented upon by the centurion,[1] and observable by us all.

The authority we need, the authority Christ appoints, is expressed in love and relationships. I say this because it is the underlying key to everything we must understand about church life and government.

Either we understand and choose to submit to the particular method of government taught in the New Testament, or we end up devising our own. There is even a small minority of Christians who allow for no leaders at all, but all this means is that by default they believe in their own authority. This is lawlessness.

---

1 Matthew 8:8-10

An Independent Eldership is at Risk

Elderships are not meant to stand alone in leadership over a city church. Where this occurs, the risks are far greater. They also, like every other expression of the Body of Christ, from individuals, to families, to Christian groups, to churches, and to the city church, are meant to be in submission, in a vital heart relationship of love and oneness, with spiritual leaders. This is spiritual covering, a crucial expression of the oneness of the Body, and an essential lifeline for grace and power.

Elderships are no different. Elderships should not expect to have authority if they themselves are not subject to authority. Otherwise, they are not positioned to experience *apostolic* life, and not actually functioning in *apostolic* authority, but in some other, more base, authority (the same applies to apostles and prophets, but that is not our subject at the moment). No eldership can be a law unto itself. There must be accountability, and an effective, vibrant means for its protection, correction, and inspiration. There must be a higher leadership they respect.

Of the fact that there are indeed risks for the eldership that goes it alone, we have a poignant example in the New Testament.

The Ephesian Example

We find it in the words of the apostle Paul, when he shared his farewell message with the Ephesian elders. He knew them well, and loved them deeply. He had founded that church and lived there three years, taught publicly every day, and from there the word of God went out all through the province of Asia. Great battles were fought and won there, and later the city was the home of the apostle John, and of Mary, the mother of our Lord Jesus.

Paul's final message to the Ephesian elders is profound and moving. But in it he included the most sombre warning. Here are his words:

> *"I know that after I leave, savage wolves will*

> *come in among you and will not spare the flock. Even from your own number men will arise and distort the truth in order to draw away disciples after them. So be on your guard!"* (Acts 20:29-31a)

The critical information for us is found in Paul's words, *"after I leave,"* and the critical lesson is that, without an apostle in the role of spiritual father fulfilling the order of Christ's government for elderships and the church as a whole, even an eldership comprised of mature and experienced anointed leaders is at risk to individual independence and self-interest.

It is not only the eldership at risk when apostolic covering is removed, but the life of the city itself, and the security and well-being of the Lord's people.

Christ still appoints leaders for His people, as He has always done. And there is a growing recognition that we are in the early days of a complete reformation of the church, being brought about by the Holy Spirit. This involves, amongst other things, the restoration of apostolic leadership.

This is not a book about apostles and apostolic ministry,[2] but I here need to give the greater context of the subject we have been dealing with. It has to be understood that eldership operates most properly and biblically when they are joined[3] with Christ's apostles in meaningful and personal relationships.

The Developing Apostolic Leadership

Thus, in the coming 21st century reformed Body of Christ, the elders will be standing in God-glorifying relationships with each other, with all the fivefold ministry of their city, and with Christ's apostles and prophets. **This is the vision that Paul outlines in Ephesians 4:1-16.**

I acknowledge that the apostolic ministry being restored is not yet mature. Nor is the church yet in a place of understanding the grace of submission that the New Testament teaches, which is required for the whole church to have the power, authority,

---

2 For a biblical exposition of this subject, see my book, *The Apostolic Revelation.*
3 Ephesians 4:16

and freedom of the apostolic life we are meant to enjoy. But it is coming, and it is today's pastors and leaders who must listen to the heart of God and follow the leading of the Holy Spirit to explore the dynamics of the holy relationships called for by the Christian faith of the New Testament. And we must look to God, prayerfully, for Him to raise apostles and prophets for us.

I admit, too, that we have the current problem in these early days of too many now thinking they are apostles when they are not. I am not referring to the 'lunatic fringe' of the church, amongst whom there have always been strange claims, nor am I referring to those who are false prophets and the like. Rather, we have at this time numbers of genuine ministers of Christ, often senior people and dearly beloved, who are mistaken about their call. These are usually mature pastors, teachers, and even prophets, who, because of their success and leadership, because of the spiritual authority they may have, because people around them honour them (as they should), and because the apostolic ministry is the 'flavour of the month,' have ended up believing they are apostles, or just as often have been promoted as such by others around them. But this is in fact the error of being premature.

Yet I think it will all come clean in the wash. Give it time. We should note that most of Christ's apostles being raised, tested, and matured, are still *hidden* – and most likely in very *small* places. At the same time, many of these others who are not actually apostles are more likely gifted fivefold ministers who, in a transitional period, have the God-given vision to work for the restoration of apostles. This is what can lead them to feel they are apostles – but they are more likely forerunners for generations of apostles yet to come.

A lot more seriousness needs to be put into the question of whether someone is an apostle or not. I am not here speaking to everyone, in the sense of Revelation 2:2, but to those many leaders now styling themselves as apostles. This is holy ground, and ought to be approached with fear. Once (I remember my early years in evangelical Christianity), no-one would presume this ground. Neither today should anyone too easily take this stand, knowing the fear of the Lord. This ground is such that it requires great fear and great humility – and only God can bring someone onto this mountain. Believe me, it is a dangerous place for man to stand if he has placed himself there.

At the same time, because we are in a transitional period and are all supposed to explore this grace, mistakes and errors of judgement will be made by the Lord's covenant people. This is inevitable, since the Church must again become familiar with the doctrine of apostles and elders and the fivefold ministry, and the reformation this brings. For this, there is an especially prevalent grace that gives freedom to explore, and allows for mistakes – at this time. But I think the time is coming when the fear of the Lord will begin to bring in the balance again, and we will find that it is, after all, holy ground.

All over the world the church needs truly great pastors. Some of these will build the world's *greatest* congregations, but this does not make them apostles. The world also needs great Christian teachers, many of whom will travel, and lecture, and write books, and *hugely* influence the world – like C.S. Lewis. But they are not apostles. And the Body of Christ and all nations need Christ's greatly anointed prophets, and some of these will have world-wide influence, and participate in the confluence of great events and impact peoples – but this does not make them apostles.

Can I appeal to my brothers and sisters? Please be what you are called to be. The Body needs a truly great, focused, properly built together, fivefold ministry. Together we change the world.

But genuine apostles we will have, by the grace of God. Yet no-one may be an apostle without a specific and extraordinary calling by Christ. (It is never the appointment of man – not even in the guise of 'authoritative' Christian leaders who claim to be apostles or prophets. If you do not have a personal testimony of having been encountered by the Lord for this purpose – not just having been successful in ministry and some other leader 'felt led' to 'ordain' you to the role – then realise your calling is probably to one of the other very important, much needed, ministry roles.) More will need to be written about this vital subject.

The Benefit of *Apostolic* Government

There are other forms of authority and government in this world, but the form of authority modelled by Christ and appointed for the church is *apostolic*.

The genius of Christ's government through apostles is that it has authority without control, and power without coercion. To be genuinely apostolic is not about being authoritarian. Where we have leaders claiming to be apostles but are authoritarian or even controlling, they are not apostles. (We do often find that authoritarian control is the outcome of a gifted teacher operating under the false assumption that they are apostles.)

The two big goals for genuine apostolic leadership are to create freedom for believers, and to build them into relationships under authority without control. How does God provide leaders that can achieve both of these things? It is through the apostolic grace of fathering. He raises apostles in order to carry Christ's authority with gentleness and with the heart of true fathers. The house must have fathers – and the fact that Paul could say *"For I am the least of the apostles… by the grace of God I am what I am"*[4] and could also say *"in Christ Jesus I became your father through the gospel,"*[5] is, for Paul and all apostles, totally part and parcel of the one thing. (And the spirit of this fathering is conveyed by apostles and imparted to all other ministries, so that all leadership for the Body of Christ in turn matures as fathers in the faith.[6])

---

4 1 Corinthians 15:9-10
5 1 Corinthians 4:15
6 1 John 2:12-14

For the believers who have the benefit of having such apostolic grace in leadership, there are huge blessings. When the church has an apostolic *life*, the outcome is the enjoyment of true community, where we together are submissive in attitude, cooperative in intent, loving from the heart, trusting by experience, at peace because secure, and devoted and obedient because we are Christ's people. In such a Christian community the grace given by Christ to apostles to lead is recognised, and submission is voluntary. The freedom is real, with no demand but *"the continuing debt to love one another."*[7] And it is amazing how, in such an apostolic community, believers do not carry 'expectations' of each other. (It is by fleshly expectations of the heart that people take offence, or are judgemental of others.) Through apostolic grace God gives the *"spirit"* of *"understanding,"*[8] an anointing, the essential oil that lubricates the machinery of vital, empowered, uniquely *Christian*, church life and fellowship.[9]

Three Periods in the Preparation of the Genuine Apostle

I should explain, there are three periods in the development and bringing to maturity of those who are being made apostles.

It has always been assumed it would take a long time for grace to bring someone to the place of being an apostle. I've heard it said that it takes 20 to 30 years to make an apostle, and 10 to 20 years to make a prophet. The years will vary, and often it will be longer than this, but the overall idea is correct.

I was waking from a nap one day when I heard the Lord say, *"Get up; I have something to tell you!"* Then He began to speak even though I was still only attempting to get up. In the following I will give you the gist of what I heard. But to preface this, you need to know that for a long time I assumed that the years of my own ministry were largely to be lived in two stages – firstly a long period of preparation, in which I was in ministry

---

7 Romans 13:8
8 Isaiah 11:2, also Ephesians 1:17-18.
9 For a biblical theology of apostolic community, see my book, *Building an Apostolic People*, formerly entitled *Holy Community*.

but still learning and maturing; then later a more mature and fruitful stage in which I and others would more greatly benefit from what I had learned and had gone through. My thought was that this latter stage was the ultimate ministry for which the earlier had been a preparation.

But no, it turns out that, at least for apostles, there are in fact *three* stages in the development of their lives in ministry.

The first stage of early learning and testing is never advanced beyond unless the would-be apostle passes the tests which will determine whether he may or may not become an actual apostle. The second stage is a long period of learning how to minister as an apostle; not only how to do the things an apostle does, but especially how to think, pray, live, and serve others as an apostle – really, how to have the heart of an apostle. The third stage is when this apostle, having reached a level of greater maturity, and *if* having passed the even more difficult tests of the heart that come late in the second level, is released by Christ into the *fullness* of being an apostle. And this last level, not released to everyone, is one that *really* counts – although it still requires further growing and testing. This minister of Christ finally lives, thinks, speaks, and acts, as a true, full, and mature apostle of Christ.[10] (This is not sinless perfection, nor mistake-free leadership, but it is mature, and trustworthy. Neither Paul, Peter, nor John were mistake-free, but they were genuine apostles, bond slaves of Jesus Christ, and trustworthy stewards of the grace of God.[11])

The three stages are real, and one does not progress from one stage to the next unless the lessons have been learned, and the tests passed. Even Paul, in his maturity, declared, *"we speak as men approved by God to be entrusted with the gospel. We are not trying to please men but God, who tests our hearts"* (1 Thessalonians 2:4).

This explains a lot. It explains, for instance, why so many claim to be apostles, but are not mature, do not have a great

10 What the nature of this apostle is like I define not here, but in my book, *The Apostolic Revelation*.
11 See Chapter 10 of The Apostolic Revelation, "The Humanity of Apostles".

understanding of apostolic ministry, and do not really think like an apostle. We must realise, it is possible for someone to have a call to be an apostle, to even be seen to be ministering as an apostle, and to seem to have apostolic gifts, and yet not be an apostle at all, or at least, not yet.

The third stage, if one arrives at it, is the stage of being in the fuller maturity of the apostolic office – the kind of thing that most people imagine an apostle to be when reading the Holy Scriptures. Those who are at the earlier stages are certainly Christ's ministers. They do have an apostolic call, and they have apostolic gifts – they bring apostolic words and minister out of apostolic grace – although often with some mixture to it. The goal, however, is full maturity in the apostolic call and ministry of Christ.

There are those who do not pass the tests of stage one, and who do not become apostles, in the real sense of it, at all. And there are those who, after passing the tests, move into the initial stages of apostolic ministry, but then settle there. They might become complacent, or may grow tired of the battle, or, just as often, in their middle-years are content with what they have achieved and are still achieving, and there is no hunger to go on continually learning, growing, and seeking God. They happily maintain what they have in gifting and ministry. They are Christ's servants, they are fruitful, and He loves them and holds their work as hugely valuable. By calling and gifting these are apostles, they are faithful, they serve many, and accomplish much. They are exemplary servants of God and the church in their own right, and this is as far as the Lord desires to take them. But there are yet others, a smaller company, who are called to and willing to embrace greater pain, and in so doing become the apostles of a greater measure, of the third stage, who then are called to carry a greater grace and responsibility, along with its cost, for the sake of Christ and the church. These are the apostles we look for, and we must ask the Lord to raise them.

As already mentioned, the apostle Paul confirms the reality of these tests when he wrote, *"We are not trying to please men but God, who tests our hearts"* (1 Thessalonians 2:4), and in another place, *"I trust that you will realise that we ourselves did not fail the test"* (2 Corinthians 13:6).

I must say something about those who do not make it past level one. A few of these fail completely, and are removed from the ministry, while some who fail continue to cling to the ministry and cause hurt and alarm. And I know of someone like this.

But the rest, perhaps the majority, of those who do not pass the stage one tests, even though they do not move on *as apostles*, do remain in the ministry of Christ, still fruitful, still serving Christ and loving His people, even though not progressing to the apostolic appointment or the full understanding of it. They have an apostolic call, they have apostolic gifts and graces, and sometimes minister as apostles, but they are not really *apostles* as such. We love them, we respect them, we receive their ministry, but we should not fool ourselves into thinking that all 'apostles' are the same. There are different levels of grace, and different levels of authority, in this ministry. But hopefully, to whatever level we have attained, we are all seeking to be fruitful for Christ.

What the world needs, and we are looking for, are the greater apostles! Those who have died to self, who walk with Christ, who have the kind of hearts that great apostles have. Knowing this, we can understand Paul's great exhortations to Timothy, already in the apostolic office, to fight the good fight and go on to excellence and maturity, which we find so rich in his epistles to the younger man he loved.

Those to whom the Lord has given such grace as to bring them to the fullness of the apostolic office – these are the real apostles who must lead us. The church must, in these days, look to Christ to send us these apostles.

Who Appoints the Elders, Then?

When I speak of city elderships enjoying the fruit of heartfelt and accountable relationships with apostles, and of being under the covering of Christ through being joined with apostles, it is these mature, trustworthy, proven apostles I have in mind.

In such an outcome, elderships then are submitted to authority – Christ's appointed authority – expressed in **love and relationships**.

Notice that nowhere did Paul write to a *church,* neither a city church nor a local congregation, to give the members or leaders instructions on how to appoint elders. This is because, biblically speaking, elders are not appointed from congregations or by congregational leaders. Paul only wrote to certain individual men, Timothy and Titus, who had been given specific authority for this purpose. They happened to be the apostles that served under Paul, and he had appointed them to watch over the churches. As apostles of Christ, then, the appointing and watching over the elderships was a specific responsibility.

Not everyone today, with so many viewpoints abounding, and vested interests everywhere, will think this a great idea. But all I am pointing out is that this is the biblical position and the only model we have. And helpfully, it is also a window into the specific apostolic structure of the Body of Christ. Titus and Timothy were fulfilling the role of apostles, and it is in fulfilling that apostolic function that they guarded, and fathered, elderships.

Beyond the function of appointing elders amongst the churches, Paul also outlined the following responsibilities for apostles in the matter of governing elders: see that they are properly honoured and remunerated (1 Timothy 3:17-18), protect them from false accusation (1 Timothy 5:19), and deal with elders if they sin with a public rebuke, which also serves to warn, and thus strengthen, the other elders (1 Timothy 3:20). This guards the city, and cuts off the sin as far as being an open gate.

But as we said before, apostolic authority in laying on of hands for those to be elders would never have been used unilaterally, but born out of being part of and living amongst a vibrant community of apostolic faith. Here were maintained great heart relationships with all the leaders. They loved each other, and served one another.

And wherever you find spiritual maturity, church leaders do love one another and work together in close heart relationships. This is the only kind of genuine apostle that I know of – if we find otherwise, we should question it.

Can I prove this to you? Read again 1 Thessalonians 2:6-12:

> *"We were not looking for praise from men, not from you or anyone else.*
> *As apostles of Christ we could have been a burden to you, but we were gentle among you, like a mother caring for her little children. We loved you so much that we were delighted to share with you not only the gospel of God but our lives as well, because you had become so dear to us. Surely you remember, brothers, our toil and hardship; we worked night and day in order not to be a burden to anyone while we preached the gospel of God to you.*
> *You are witnesses, and so is God, of how holy, righteous and blameless we were among you who believed. For you know that we dealt with each of you as a father deals with his own children, encouraging, comforting and urging you to live lives worthy of God, who calls you into his kingdom and glory."*

Even more clearly, let's go to Paul's farewell speech to the Ephesian elders. It would be good to read all of Acts 20:17-38, but here are some selected verses. Read these for insight as to Paul's integrity as an apostle, and his role amongst elders. This, we will find, will be typical of all apostles to whom Christ gives any amount of greater authority in the coming days:

> 'From Miletus, Paul sent to Ephesus for the elders of the church. When they arrived, he said to them: "You know how I lived the whole time I was with you, from the first day I came into the province of Asia. I served the Lord with great humility and with tears, although I was severely tested by the plots of the Jews." ' (Acts 20:17-19)

> "However, I consider my life worth nothing to me, if only I may finish the race and complete the task the Lord Jesus has given me–the task of testifying to the gospel of God's grace." (Acts 20:24)

> "I have not coveted anyone's silver or gold or clothing. You yourselves know that these hands of mine have supplied my own needs and the needs of my companions. In everything I did, I showed you that by this kind of hard work we must help the weak, remembering the words the Lord Jesus himself said: 'It is more blessed to give than to receive.'
> When he had said this, he knelt down with all of them and prayed. They all wept as they embraced him and kissed him. What grieved them most was his statement that they would never see his face again. Then they accompanied him to the ship." (Acts 20:33-38)

Yet at this time we are still in a very formative period, and everything is in transition. It might be that, in this early period of exploring eldership, a search for formation must take place from within, by the pastors of each city building their lives together in honouring and loving relationships, and by the potential elders coming to the fore in that fellowship of love and respect.

If this occurs, even when the eldership so established is functional and effective, there is still a crucial role for apostles. And if the place of apostles is avoided, or neglected, then at best the eldership risks just muddling along, but at worst, serious failures.

The worst of these failures, as we saw earlier, was to come for the Ephesian elders. Let's look again at the passage found in Acts 20:28-31, with Paul's telling perspective in verse 29 here underlined:

> *"Keep watch over yourselves and all the flock of which the Holy Spirit has made you overseers. Be shepherds of the church of God, which he bought with his own blood. I know that <u>after I leave</u>, savage wolves will come in among you and will not spare the flock. Even from your own number men will arise and distort the truth in order to draw away disciples after them. So be on your guard! Remember that for three years I never stopped warning each of you night and day with tears."*

Taking our cue from the word of Paul, *"I know that after I leave,"* we saw earlier that when you remove the covering apostle, you no longer have in place the very important component needed with respect to keeping an eldership healthy, alive, humble, and servant-hearted, guarded in the truth as well as in heart-motive.

The Covering of Apostles over the Eldership

It should be said that not every city needs to have a resident apostle, and it is a mistake to operate with this as an inflexible view – otherwise you would have to conclude that every town and village must have, on that basis, a resident apostle also.

This is to misunderstand the nature of the apostolic ministry.

Sometimes, apostles will be resident as part of the eldership, as was the case of the original church in Jerusalem,[12] and sometimes the city eldership will be comprised of prophets and teachers, as was the case with Antioch,[13] who related to apostolic covering provided by the apostles of Jerusalem.[14] City churches of the future may fruitfully have either arrangement, with resident apostles in the eldership when available, or an eldership comprised of available qualified fivefold ministers – but either way, both must of biblical necessity maintain spiritual order and the effectiveness of Christ's government through vibrant heart relationship with external covering apostles. (In addition, there will be many apostles in travelling ministry. Churches everywhere should receive the visiting ministry Christ sends, so as to be healthy. We all need to receive apostles, prophets, evangelists, pastors and teachers to give an outside input of grace, wisdom, instruction, and impartation. Every church needs to receive the blessing of such ministry, in particular the commanded blessing given by apostles.)

There will be many cities whose eldership functions very well with a team of prophets and teachers, as in Antioch. The bigger the city the more likely it may be to have one or more apostles resident therein, but that does not make such an apostle necessarily part of the local eldership. If he's a local, he might become one of the elders, he might even be the leader of the team, but he should never be considered an automatic inclusion for membership. Nor should he be, if local, the *apostolic covering* for that particular eldership. You cannot be your own spiritual covering.

Every such eldership, then, must relate to an apostle (or a team of apostles) from outside the city. In other words, the eldership itself, including its apostles if any, must have an apostolic covering that is **external and independent of the**

12 Acts 15:2,4
13 Acts 13:1
14 Acts 11:22,27

city, with whom they will walk in transparent accountability and heartfelt relationships. They must relate to fathers who will love them.

Three Levels of Spiritual Covering

There are, in fact, three levels of covering over the Body of Christ. Here is not the place to explore them, but I will briefly outline them.

Firstly, there is a spiritual covering that the senior minister and the ministry team provide over a local church congregation. In any given ministry, someone will have the primary anointing of authority and responsibility before God for that work, and must build the leadership team together in unity, holiness, and love. This then can, and does when properly established, provide a wonderful spiritual covering for their people, which is very powerful. Local congregational leaders standing as one with their ministers are hugely important for the security and well-being of local churches and families. But this does not do enough for cities, and we all have to live in the cities, not just in our homes and church fellowships. And our kids grow up in these cities. We can do more!

The second, then, is what we are speaking of in this book – the powerful spiritual covering that can be established over whole cities and regions through effective, holy, New Testament eldership. That is the way our cities and families are to be made all the more secure, and made to 'prosper' in the biblical sense. This covering has, of course, been largely missing. The key is the oneness of the Body, and of the spiritual leadership over that Body, in each place.

The third is the *apostolic* covering, a powerful and extensive *spiritual* covering indeed, which the church must now come to understand, value highly, desire, and embrace. In this day, however, when not much else has been built, there are those of us who relate directly to apostles, and they become the covering of Christ for our individual churches. I know of various pastors, both denominational and independent, who are benefitting greatly from having embraced these relationships of love, trust, and fathering grace.

But apostolic covering is meant to have far greater outcomes than this. Apostolic covering is a grace meant to be established over cities, states, nations, and indeed over the whole world. The Scriptures speak of such a grace, seen in Isaiah 4:5, *"over all the glory will be a canopy,"* and Jesus told His Father He had given us the *"glory"* that He had been given *"so that we might be one."*[15] The unity (oneness) of the church is the outworking of that glory, and He promised there would be a *"canopy"* over it. No wonder the Psalmist wrote, *"How good... it is when brothers dwell together in unity...for there the Lord commands the blessing"* Psalm 133:1,3. We are told, moreover, that *"he who sits on the throne will spread his tent over them"* (Revelation 7:15). Psalm 5:11-12 speaks also of this shield to be established for the protection of the righteous.

To achieve this, the lives of those apostles raised by Christ to great authority for this purpose must be joined at the heart. It is based on relationship alone – apostles one-at-heart, walking together the way Peter and John did in the early days of the Jerusalem church, and as did Paul and Timothy. Moses and Joshua, and Elijah and Elisha are other examples of this oneness. They were close companions in ministry, from the heart.

But in coming days it will be greater. And the model is the relationship that Jesus had with His Father in the days of His ministry.[16] How do we know? Jesus said so! That we would find that relationship He made part of His high priestly prayer:

> *"My prayer is not for them alone. I pray also for those who will believe in me through their message, that all of them may be one, Father, just as you are in me and I am in you. May they also be in us so that the world may believe that you have sent me. I have given them the glory that you gave me, that*

15 John 17:22
16 For a biblical theology of this relationship, see my book, The Spirit of Sonship.

*they may be one as we are one: I in them and you in
me. May they be brought to complete unity to let the
world know that you sent me and have loved them
even as you have loved me."* (John 17:20-23)

Pastors and churches who now purposefully relate to
apostles have already begun to experience the blessings of such
covering over their work.

Apostolic Covering

One Sunday morning in 1999, as the senior leader at Peace,
but in accord with my pastoral team and other leaders, I prayed
and established 'officially' for the first time that we had an
accountable relationship with an apostle of Christ. In the Lord
we received the blessing of that relationship as an apostolic
covering, and I released it over the church.

The wonderful thing was that in that moment, spontaneous
healings took place in the congregation. It seemed to
immediately repair what had been broken a few years before
with the division of the old eldership.

What I had not realised in the earlier years, but came
to understand much later, was that when I first formed the
eldership, in 1988, we were, as a church, still operating under
the old pastoral/teaching anointing of the denominational
method. It was still, of course, a blessing and it seemed to work,
but something had been going on causing change that we didn't
anticipate. For in our prayers we had been crying out to God
to get us on the cutting edge of whatever He was doing in the
world.

In answering that prayer, things were changing around us
and in us, and one of the direct outcomes was that we were
being brought into prophetic and apostolic grace. The apostolic
anointing, along with prophetic grace, became the primary
anointing over the church. What we didn't realise was that this
would require, in time, a different way of operating, and really,

an altogether different way of thinking. And this is happening all over the world.

The main outworking of these apostolic and prophetic graces is found, as it was always meant to be, in our understanding of relationships! Specifically, how we walk with our leaders and our leaders with us – and crucially, how leaders walk with each other – in the fellowship of the Holy Spirit.[17] There is just one feast that the New Testament commands us to keep, and that is: the daily feast of Christian fellowship,[18] (which, of course, is centred in, and draws power from, the table of the Lord).

The old system is anachronistic, and the Spirit of God in these years is trying to move us all on to completely better things. These 'better things' intended for us are those spoken of by our Lord Jesus in His high priestly prayer, then by Paul in his vision of the future of the church as outlined in Ephesians 4:1-16, which followed on from his own prayer for *"all the saints,"* a prayer begun in Ephesians 1:17-19a and completed in Ephesians 3:16-19.

The nub of both those prayers, which must be answered on earth and in time (not when time is over), and the outcome of Paul's teaching (effectively a prophecy of the future of the church on earth in this age) is this:

> Christ's church on earth will be brought to a more mature state of grace, based on love and understanding, which Paul calls, respectively, *"the measure of all the fullness of God"*[19] and *"the whole measure of the fullness of Christ,"*[20] and the Lord calls it *"complete unity."*[21] Jesus defines this state of grace, which Paul called *"maturity,"*[22] in terms of us all being one in the same way as God the Father and God the Son are One![23] Our Lord

17 1 John 1:3
18 1 Corinthians 5:8
19 Ephesians 3:19
20 Ephesians 4:13
21 John 17:23
22 Ephesians 4:13
23 John 17:21,22,23

Jesus went on to pray for this to occur so that the world will believe[24] the gospel.

Dearly beloved, this is our future! It is worth striving for! The goal is Christ-likeness, and the prize is life.

---

24 John 17:21, 23

In Conclusion

Some Thoughts for All Believers

Take seriously the need for your pastor to do something about this call to build the oneness of the ministry and the church. Pray for them, encourage them, stand with them, give them time and opportunity to build city relationships, walk with them in it, and help them lead your church where you need to go as a people. Highly value your leaders, and honour them.

There is for you a great word of Scripture, and you can be the 'preacher' of it: *"Now we ask you, brothers, to respect those who work hard among you, who are over you in the Lord and who admonish you. Hold them in the highest regard in love because of their work. Live in peace with each other"* (1 Thessalonians 5:12-13).

Some Thoughts for Christ's Appointed Leaders

Bishops, Pastors, Denominational leaders, and local church leaders, let us all build relationships at another level – that of the *heart*. We can no longer afford to be estranged from each other along denominational lines.

Pastors themselves must want, and cry out for, a new deal. It is primarily in their interaction with each other that this re-forming must be worked out. The whole structure of the church across the world must be changed. There is a better way, and it is *biblical*.

Fortunately, the Holy Spirit is at work, and reformation is underway. Allow the Lord to lead the rearrangement, and work with Him – He is going to rearrange things anyway.

Pastors will need to begin a long conversation. It takes time to explore relationships, develop trust, grow in love, and feel a great sense of belonging to each other. But it will begin with the inner realisation that love for both the city and the Body of Christ are amongst the great foundational criteria for genuine leadership ministry – but this love, if genuine, has its first outworking in commitment to and love for the other fivefold ministers around us.

And in every place, some of the ministers, at least four or five I would think, will need to realise they are committed to the one city for life. Under denominational thinking, this has not been a value, and often not allowed. But it is quite essential to the greater outworking of the Lord's purposes and every city's need. Christ will make this clear to those so called in every place, but the concept has to be enunciated or it doesn't make it onto the radar of our values when it has been obliterated by tradition.

Understanding the Ways of God

The Scriptures in many places urge us to gain understanding, and Psalm 49:10-20 warns of the outcomes of life and the consequences for not understanding.

Sometimes spiritual leaders forget that the words, *"a man who has riches without understanding"* (v20), and its consequences, might apply to them as much as anyone else if they do not put the Lord's house and family above their own interests of self-promotion or denominational priority. Men praise them while they live, as the Psalm says, and they appear to have *"wealth"* and *"splendour,"* but they, like all, go to the grave and are soon forgotten. And almost everything they did and said is forgotten. Only if we *"build"* with *"gold,"*[1] will our *"deeds follow"*[2] us. My understanding is that to build with gold means to live and minister under authority, that of Christ.

Unity, Love, and Oneness from the Leaders Down

Every pastor preaches for unity and love in his congregation, but very often doesn't think to apply the same standards to himself in relation to the other pastors in Christian leadership across the city/town/region. But in fact, that is where these truths *first* apply. Jesus taught His twelve these values and standards, not in the first instance for them to teach others, but rather to instruct them how they must function amongst themselves. And Jesus applied it as a higher principle upon those who would be the leaders of leaders: *'Jesus called the Twelve and said, "If anyone wants to be first, he must be the very last, and the servant of all" '* (Mark 9:35).

No More Crazy Stuff

I remember in 1989, when asking the leader of one of the churches to meet with others and build respect and relationships, the reply was, "I have been called to build *this* church. I don't care what other pastors are doing, I am only called to make *this* church great." In 1989, that might have seemed to many an arguable position, but actually it is untenable. Rather, it is those whose hearts are for what the Lord wants for *all* His people, and who yearn for the progress of the *whole* church, that understand the true nature of the ministry of Christ. But the kinds of problems we have all over the world that come from striving and competition, or independence, or from denominational division, need to be seen as being ridiculously crazy for real spiritual leaders, and cannot be the church *biblically*. It is nothing like what Jesus taught, or Paul insisted upon.

---

1   1 Corinthians 3:12, Revelation 3:18
2   Revelation 14:13

Apostles, Too, as One

Apostles, too, as they become established, will need to come into fruitful unity, as one before Christ. In the past, we have seen relational networks of churches. Now is coming the time for relational networks of *apostles*. But not built as an institution! Please: it must be a *personal* network, built by means of healthy, loving, committed, *personal relationships*, involving leaders of the 'willing to lay down your life for your brother' kind, rather than the 'building your own kingdom' type. It is *hearts* that must be knit together. Christ alone they must serve, and they must hold each other dear.

To Close, Some Thoughts from the Teaching of Watchman Nee

The following are selected passages from Pages 146-148 of Watchman Nee's *The Normal Christian Life*, Third Edition 1961, published by Victory Press, London.

"The vessel through which the Lord Jesus can reveal himself in this generation is not the individual but the Body. True, 'God hath dealt to each man a measure of faith' (Romans 12:3), but alone in isolation man can never fulfil God's purpose. It requires a complete Body to attain to the stature of Christ and to display his glory. Oh that we might really see this!"

"Let me stress that this is not just a comfortable thought. It is a vital factor in the life of God's people. We cannot get along without one another. That is why fellowship in prayer is so important. Prayer together brings in the help of the Body, as must be clear from Matthew 18:19, 20. Trusting the Lord by myself may not be enough. I must trust him with others. I must learn to pray 'Our Father...' on the basis of oneness with the Body, for without the help of the Body I cannot get through. Alone I cannot serve the Lord effectively, and he will spare no pains to teach me this. He will bring things to an end, allowing doors to close and leaving me knocking my head against a blank wall until I realize that I need the help of the Body as well as of the Lord. For the life of Christ is the life of the Body, and his gifts are given to us for work that builds up the Body.

"The Body is not an illustration but a fact."

"This is the very opposite of man's condition by nature. In Adam I have the life of Adam, but that is essentially individual. There is no union, no fellowship in sin, but only self-interest and distrust of others. As I go on with the Lord I soon discover, not only that the problem of sin and of my natural strength has to be dealt with, but that there is also a further problem created by my 'individual' life, the life that is sufficient in itself and does not recognize its need for and union in the Body. I might have got over the problems of sin and the flesh, and yet still be a confirmed individualist..."

"Yes, the cross must do its work here, reminding me that in Christ I have died to that old life of independence which I inherited from Adam, and that in resurrection I have become not just an individual believer in Christ but a member of His Body. There is a vast difference between the two. When I see this, I shall at once have done with independence and shall seek fellowship. The life of Christ in me will gravitate to the life of Christ in others. I can no longer take an individual line. Jealousy will go. Competition will go. Private work will go. My interests, my ambitions, my preferences, all will go. It will no longer matter which of us does the work. All that will matter will be that the Body grows."

"Only the Holy Spirit can bring this home to us... but when He does it will revolutionize our life and work."

For other great resources by
John Alley see the following pages.

The Apostolic Revelation

The Reformation of the Church

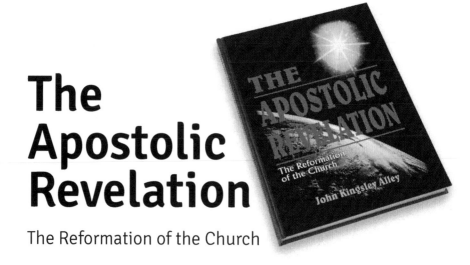

God is progressively releasing into the earth powerful apostolic and prophetic anointings, and is restoring the apostolic nature of the church itself! Every Christian needs to prayerfully consider the message of this book, and hear what the Spirit is saying to the church. The change is ongoing, and God is acting in the history of the church and nations.

The Apostolic Revelation unveils a series of dynamic concepts that are crucial to the life of the church and the restoration of its apostolic power. It establishes benchmarks for the apostolic ministry, and gives definition to the apostolic structure of the church. Here is a revelation of apostolic methods, and God's heart for the church and its leadership. In this study, today's apostolic message is harmonised with and grounded in the apostolic revelation of Christ given to Paul, the apostle to the Gentiles.

This work is the result of 13 years of inquiry, searching the mind of the Spirit regarding the place of apostles today, and seeking to understand what it means for the church to be the mature apostolic church. Apostolic grace is for every believer. This book seeks to equip you to receive a greater grace, and prepare you for the astounding days ahead.

The Spirit of Sonship

An Apostolic Grace

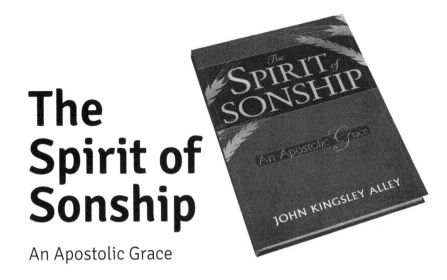

The "spirit of sonship" is an apostolic grace which brings about the spiritual maturity of the believer, the revival of apostolic Christianity, and ultimately, the maturity of the church.

This important book reveals that the values and heart attitudes of what we may call the spirit of sonship is the very nature and essence of authentic apostolic New Testament Christianity.

You will discover a fresh approach to understanding and walking in grace, through relationships. The subject is huge, and wonderful; the whole of the Scriptures and all of salvation history must now be seen in the light of *sonship* and its implications.

"You are about to glean from a man who's been on an incredible journey of revelation and discovery. I know of no other book published on this subject that is so biblical, inspiring, and practical." Rev. Dr. John McElroy

Building An Apostolic People

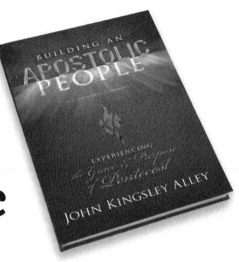

Experiencing the Grace and Purpose of Pentecost

The powerful teaching developed in this book began with a revelation the Lord gave concerning The Spirit of Understanding - a Biblical anointing that enables a church to become a people of one heart and mind. This is the grace that was poured out on the day of Pentecost, when, with the coming of the Holy Spirit, the disciples were changed from individuals with selfish ambition and petty jealousies, to a Christian community of deep love and agreement. This great anointing in Pentecost is what is required for the Church today to again be such a people of one heart and mind - a holy and apostolic people.

"There is a sense of peace and order and a flow of grace that has modelled to me an understanding of the revelations of which John teaches and writes about in his books. These revelations are genuinely outworked in the daily life of his family and community." Jenny Hagger AM Australian House of Prayer for All Nations

Purchase John Alley's books from
www.amazon.com or peace.org.au/shop

Other great resources
are available free

www.peace.org.au

Listen/Download recent messages
Watch video messages

Peace Apostolic Ministries

POSTAL ADDRESS:
PO Box 10187, Frenchville QLD 4701, Australia

OFFICE ADDRESS:
8 Thozet Rd, Koongal QLD 4701, Australia

PHONE: +61 (07) 4926-9911
FAX: +61 (07) 4926-9944

EMAIL: mail@peace.org.au
WEB: peace.org.au

Made in the USA
San Bernardino, CA
01 December 2016